C000075776

Horse of a Different Colour

Horse of a Different Colour

by

MELODIE TRUDUEAX

First Published in 2015 by Fantastic Books Publishing

Cover design by Heather Murphy

ISBN: 978-1-909163-89-8 (electronic)
ISBN: 978-1-909163-90-4 (print)

DEDICATION

For having taken part in one of mankind's greatest and coolest of adventures, this book is dedicated to astronauts. Firstly to Helen Sharman who I met many many years ago in Banner Cross (she won't remember me but I won't forget her) and also to the two-hundred-and-twenty-one who have visited the International Space Station – that's one-hundred-and-thirty-six from NASA, forty-four from Roscosmos, sixteen from ESA (including Tim Peake, the first Briton up there), seven from JAXA, six from CSA, one from CNES, one from AEB, one from ANGKASA, one from KARI, one from KazCosmos and seven space tourists – at the time of publication.

ACKNOWLEDGEMENTS

My thanks go to the team at Fantastic Books Publishing for their support; to the editors for being relentless in forcing me out of plot holes, to the copyeditors and proof readers for catching my typos and to CEO Dan Grubb for taking on my vision and letting me run with it.

My thanks also to Tony Bradman, one of the greats of modern children's writing, for taking time out of his busy schedule to read my words, give me his advice and for liking my book.

CHAPTER 1

Chocolate and Grass

'Get up, Megan Crewe. This is where you get off.'

Megan felt her arms gripped as she was hauled out of her seat and dragged down the bus.

'Get off me, Naylor O'Neill,' she screeched. 'This isn't my stop.'

As she struggled and fought, Megan glimpsed Naylor's face, red and contorted, as her captor screamed, 'Grab her legs. She's kicking me.'

Strong arms closed on Megan and bustled her down the aisle. There was nothing she could do. Now that Naylor was bus monitor, she and her gang decided where people got off. And it was no good appealing to the bus driver. He just snapped bad words and muttered, 'Kids!' to himself.

Megan called out anyway, 'Amy! Help me,' and heard a loud burst of laughter from Naylor. Well, I suppose I deserved that, she thought as they pushed her off the bus and into the lane. Naylor was the strongest girl in the class. No way Amy could stand up to her.

Naylor's grinning face looked out at her as the doors swung shut. This was all because Naylor had heard her say she thought the lane was creepy, and now she'd have to walk all the way down it on her own.

She pulled herself to her feet and bashed her hands down her skirt and sweatshirt. It would be even more unfair if she ended up in trouble for messing up her school clothes.

As the bus swept off, she caught a glimpse of Amy being pushed back into her seat. Good old Amy for trying to get off too, but she hadn't hope against Naylor's gang.

No one was about, and despite the sunshine, the lane felt cool. 'I don't care about walking down here on my own,' Megan announced to the world, but her voice sounded thin.

She hadn't gone more than a metre before a sound caught her attention. The pad-pad-pad of soft footsteps following her.

She spun round. The lane lay empty behind her. Gritting her teeth she strode on, head held high. No creepy old lane was going to scare her. That whisper of footfalls was just her imagination. And that sound like heavy breathing was just the rustle of the breeze.

She gulped and speeded up. I'm not scared of a silly old lane … I'm not scared of a silly old lane, she said over and over in her head.

But as she sped along, her hand rummaged in her pocket for her phone. If she rang Amy, it would be like having someone here with her. Of course, it would only work if Amy had her phone. Megan crossed her fingers for luck on that one. Amy was the most phone-forgetful person she'd ever known. Except for Amy's mum who was just as bad. Amy's dad was always pulling at his hair and shouting things like, 'I'm surprised you've remembered your own heads!'

Then a wonderful thing happened. Instead of closing on her phone, Megan's hand met something far nicer at the bottom of her pocket. The chocolate bar she and Amy had bought to eat on the way home. She'd kept it hidden while Naylor was around, and it was too bad about Amy who wouldn't get any now, but she would understand. Eating chocolate would drive scary noises right out of her head. She stopped to pull it out.

… pad … pad … pad…

The chocolate bar was in her hand before she realised. Footsteps! Those weren't imaginary. They were loud and clear and coming closer.

With a squeal of shock, Megan identified the sound of someone following her just the other side of the hedge.

Then she was sprinting down the lane as fast as she'd ever run, her heart pounding. The footsteps were no longer soft. They thundered after her from behind the hawthorn.

The thick hedge only lasted as far as the gate at the end. And when she reached it, Megan knew she would be face to face with … it …

But there was nowhere else to run. This was the way home. Her heart hammered as the gate approached. With a gasp of horror, she glimpsed an enormous head … huge eyes …

She couldn't outrun it. It had got there first.

Megan threw herself to the ground and buried her face in her hands. Cowering, she waited for the touch of a soul-sucking Dementor.

3

Nothing happened.

Warily, she opened one eye and looked up. The long face peered down from over the gate.

A wave of relief flooded through her and she pulled herself to her feet. It was only the horse that lived in the field.

'Oh, Jack, you threadbare old nag! What were you doing scaring me like that?' She pointed her finger at him and tried to be stern, but she was so pleased he wasn't a demon, she couldn't help smiling.

Jack had lived in this field forever. Megan's mother used to lift her up to pat him when she was very little, but she hadn't been past this way for ages.

'I didn't know you could run that fast,' she told him. 'I thought you were too old.'

In reply, Jack whinnied, bending his head sideways to cast a longing glance at the chocolate clutched in Megan's hand.

'Do you like chocolate, Jack?'

It was funny, but Megan felt she wanted to eat something springy and fresh like the lush green grass hanging from Jack's mouth. It seemed like juicy blades of grass would taste far better than chocolate. Maybe her mother was right. Maybe you did get to like sprouts as you got older.

'Swap you a piece of chocolate for some grass,' she said, laughing.

But something very peculiar stopped the laugh.

She gasped as the field opened up before her. She could

see too much of it. It was like looking both ways at once. Her eyes were in the wrong place. She panicked and tried to get away. But that made things worse. She had forgotten how to run. It was too complicated.

'I've got too many legs,' she wailed.

Everything tangled. She felt herself falling.

And as she landed in the mud, she heard Amy's voice. 'Megan. Megan.'

'Amy?'

Megan lifted her head. Amy had got away from Naylor and come back for her. Good old Amy. But yuk! What was this horrible taste? She was lying in the mud, face down. Her mouth was full of grass.

And there was Amy, running towards her.

'What happened, Megan? Did you fall?'

'I … I'm not sure.'

'Come on, Megan,' Amy urged. 'Let's get going. That awful man's over there.'

'What awful man?'

'Naylor's uncle.'

Megan stood up and turned to look. There was Nathan O'Neill at the far side of the field standing staring, but not at them. He was staring at Jack, who was churning the grass in an effort to get to his feet, and as covered in mud as Megan was.

'What's up with Jack?' Megan said.

'I don't know.' Amy cast anxious eyes towards Nathan O'Neill. 'He just fell over.'

'What do you mean, just fell over?'

Amy glanced at the horse. 'It was like he was trying to balance on his front legs. He fell on his face. Come on, Megan. Let's run. Naylor's uncle gives me the creeps.'

'Hey!' Megan was indignant, 'Jack's got silver paper in his mouth. He's got our chocolate.'

'Come on, Megan. Run!'

CHAPTER 2

Grass and Chocolate

For the rest of the week, Naylor and her gang left Megan and Amy alone. It was a relief to Megan, but at the same time she couldn't help wondering what would happen if she was forced to go back home again down that lane.

That strange business with Jack … the grass … and the chocolate. She told herself she must have imagined it.

But when the weekend came, she simply had to check.

I'll do a scientific test, she told herself as she headed first for the shop, where her hand hovered over the sweet rack. One of her favourite solid chocolate bars or something cheaper? After all, her experiment might mean losing some of it. She compromised on a Kit Kat and handed her money over the counter to Mrs Clover.

'Be sure and put the paper in the bin outside,' Mrs Clover told her.

'I'm not eating it now. I'm saving it for an experiment.'

Mrs Clover laughed. 'Not eating it now? I'll believe that when I see it.'

'I once kept a packet of Maltesers a whole week,' Megan said, and hurried out before Mrs Clover asked any questions. She hadn't told a lie. The packet had dropped down the grating at the side of the house and it had taken a week to find a way to fish it out.

It was hard to ignore a Kit Kat in her pocket, but she was determined, and she arrived at the gate of the field with the wrapper still untouched.

'Now we'll see what happens,' she said, taking it out. With a ripping of paper and a deft snap, she freed half a chocolate finger and laid it on top of the gate. Then she bent down to pull up a tuft of grass that she balanced next to the chocolate.

'Have some nice juicy grass, Megan,' she invited herself, and at once felt her mouth do that shape it did when her mother said, eat your sprouts, Megan. No, there was no way she could think of eating grass while that crunchy chocolate sat next to it.

That was part one of the experiment over. She brushed the tuft of grass back to the ground and popped the piece of chocolate in her mouth. As it was only half a finger, it was gone in a moment so she snapped off another piece and ate that too.

The dark silky flavour filled her mouth as she crunched and swallowed, climbing over the gate and setting off across the field. And that was the problem with a Kit Kat over say a Dairy Milk or a Yorkie. With solid chocolate, you could let it melt on your tongue, let the taste linger, although the way it softened round the edges, it usually forced you to slurp the liquidy bit down your throat and bite into the rest. But with a Kit Kat you simply couldn't risk all the chocolate melting away or you'd be left with just plain biscuit.

If she hadn't been so determined to see this test through, all four fingers would have been gone before she was halfway across the grassy expanse, but she rewrapped the last one tightly and pushed it into her pocket. The first part of the experiment had worked fine. She'd presented herself with a piece of chocolate and a tuft of grass. Now she must do the same with Jack. Trust him to be at the wrong end of the field.

'Here you are, Jack.' She held out her offerings on an outstretched hand.

The enormous lips snaked down. Megan held her breath in anticipation, and in just a little fear for her fingers. Hot breath from the huge hairy nostrils rippled her sleeve. Jack brushed aside the chocolate and extended his lips to engulf the grass.

'There. Just as I thought.' She gave a nod of satisfaction, and inspected the final chocolate finger.

'Well, thanks very much. That's in a sorry state. You've got horse spit all over my Kit Kat.'

She crouched in the long grass, and was wiping the chocolate clean on a dock leaf when she heard voices. From out between Jack's legs, she could see the old man who looked after things at the big house walking towards the field with Naylor's uncle, Nathan O'Neill.

'No, Mr O'Neill,' the man was saying, 'we've never rented out this stretch of meadow. See, there's only this bit and old Mr Garside always said he wanted Jack to have it, for his retirement like. And that's what we did.'

'There'll be no room for passengers once the place is mine,' O'Neill said. 'You'll have to take him with you.'

'I've nowhere for him, Mr O'Neill.'

'Well then, sell him.'

'Oh, I couldn't do that. He's quite an age, you see. No one'll want him for riding out, not at his age. It's a shame because there's life in him yet. But that's how it is.'

'He's your problem, not mine. I'm buying enough trouble with this property as it is. I don't need hangers on.'

'Just you let him graze this bit of meadow. He's no trouble and I'll come and see to his few needs.'

Mr O'Neill seemed to blow out a long breath and grit his teeth. 'Look, if I don't buy this place, it'll go to rack and ruin and the bank'll take it. It'll be hard enough making it pay its way, and this is prime building land. The nag has to go.'

'But Mr O'Neill ...'

'But nothing. If the place is repossessed, the nag'll be shipped out to the glue factory or sold on for dog meat.'

The old man looked shocked. 'Mr O'Neill, you'll have to take him over when you buy the place. We can't let him go to the knacker man.'

It seemed to Megan that O'Neill stopped to pull in another deep breath before he clapped his hand on the old man's arm. His voice was friendly now, but Megan could see a hard glint in his eye. 'Well, well, I'm sure we'll find a way. I know you wouldn't sell him for dog meat.'

The old man squared his shoulders and marched on.

Before following him, O'Neill turned and gave Jack a sardonic stare.

Megan's heart did a back flip. She thought he'd spotted her. But no, it was Jack he was looking at. 'He wouldn't sell you for dog meat, you old bag of bones,' Megan heard him mutter, 'but I will.'

Jack and Megan watched O'Neill and the old man as they pushed their way through the gate and into the top of Jack's field.

Realisation and fury built inside Megan. Mr O'Neill, whose worst sin to date was to have Naylor for a niece, was plotting treachery. He was going to buy Jack along with the big house. And he was going to send him to the knacker man. She looked up at Jack and saw big trusting eyes follow the two men as they walked away.

There wasn't time to feel afraid. Megan would show Mr O'Neill once and for all. She would make things all right for Jack.

In a moment she was up and bounding across towards the two men. She scarcely had time to worry what her mother would say about her being caught trespassing, and no time at all to wonder at how quickly she ate up the distance between herself and O'Neill.

There was one delicious moment of triumph, of seeing terror on O'Neill's face as he turned and scrambled over the fence. She skidded up an inch behind him, crashed into the wooden spars, and heard the timber groan.

The fence was a stout one. It held firm.

O'Neill was cowering, but safe. The old man rushed up to him. 'By heck, Mr O'Neill, I've never seen him act like that before. Are you all right?'

Him, thought Megan wildly, never seen him act like that? She looked down at her brown furry legs, at her muddy hooves. She had to bend her head sideways. And in the wide sweep of landscape now visible to her, she saw herself a long way off sitting contentedly in the long grass, chewing something.

In her other eye's field of vision was Nathan O'Neill, getting to his feet, wiping the mud from his coat, a look of fury suffusing his features.

The feeling of triumph drained away. Far from making it all right, Megan realised she'd made things worse than ever for Jack.

CHAPTER 3

Chocolate as an aid to thinking

When Megan arrived home panting and breathless, she rushed straight to her mother. 'Mr O'Neill ... big house ... buying it ... Jack the horse. We mustn't let him.'

'Megan!' her mother roared. 'What on earth have you been up to? Those clothes were clean on this morning.'

'Oh Mum, that's not important.' Megan jigged up and down. Grown-ups simply had no grasp of priorities. 'We have to stop Mr O'Neill buying Jack.'

'It's easy for you to say it's not important. It isn't you who has all the washing and ironing to do.' Megan's mother let out a big sigh, then gave a smile. 'I'd forgotten about Jack. You used to love that horse when you were little. You were always asking to visit him. Then one day you didn't want to any more. And yes, I'd heard that Mr O'Neill was buying the place. It's a good job he is, or it would go to rack and ruin. But he won't be buying Jack as well. They'll find a good home for him, I'm sure. Now go upstairs and get your other trousers on. I want to get the mud out of those before it bakes on.'

'No, but he is, Mum. He's going to buy the house and Jack. We've got to do something.'

'Why this sudden interest? You never bothered about horses after you stopped wanting to visit Jack. You didn't even want riding lessons that time Amy started going to the stables.'

That was true. It had always been Naylor and her friends who paraded their prize-winning ponies. 'No, but Mum, it's not fair. They're going to leave Jack for Mr O'Neill to look after and he's going to send him straight to the glue factory.'

'Oh Megan, of course he won't. What on earth makes you think he'd do that?'

Megan opened her mouth to speak and then realised the difficulty of explaining the full circumstances to her mother. 'Well, he would,' she said. 'He's as bad as Naylor. I'm off to find Amy. She'll have some ideas.'

'Not so fast. You're getting out of those muddy clothes before you go anywhere.'

Sometimes, there was no point in trying to argue with a grown-up. It was just a waste of time, and Megan had no time to spare, so she rushed upstairs to do as she was told.

Clean and neat, muddy clothes delivered to the kitchen, Megan set off at a run. And as she raced along towards Amy's, the spark of an idea began to form.

Amy had a cousin. Megan couldn't recall his name, but she remembered him as a sensible sort of person. She and Amy had once found his coat lying over the sofa with a packet of tiny crunchy chocolate biscuits peeping out of the pocket. Really, they'd only meant to eat one each, because after all, the packet was open and out in plain sight where anyone might have spotted it. He hadn't minded at all when he came in and found them quarrelling over how to share out the last one. He'd even shown them how to make it fair. The problem was that he'd moved away. Far away. In fact, he'd emigrated to the other side of the world.

But the germ of the idea was still there, and even if it came to nothing, Amy would think of something. She was good at ideas.

'You know that cousin of yours, Amy?' Megan greeted her. 'The one who went to Australia? Do you think he'd like an extra horse?'

'Not at the moment. He had an accident and got injured so they've got to move. They're selling their animals not getting new ones.'

Megan's face fell. She'd been sure Amy's cousin was the solution. It might have been a bit of hassle getting Jack to Australia, but they could probably have found a way to put him on a boat. After all, animals did travel about. Race horses even went in aeroplanes.

'Anyway, why?' Amy wanted to know. 'You haven't got a horse.'

Megan told her.

'Mr O'Neill wouldn't do that.' Amy was shocked.

'He would. He's as bad as Naylor.'

'But Megan, he wouldn't have him turned into glue when he promised not to.'

'You're as bad as my mum. I tell you he would. Jack

15

chased him and made him fall over in the mud. He's mad as anything.'

'That old horse? He never chases anyone.'

Megan hesitated. 'Well, it sort of wasn't him. It's a bit kind of difficult to explain. It was me.'

'You chased Mr O'Neill? Oh Megan, how could you?'

'He thought it was the horse.' Megan looked at Amy's disbelieving face. So much for Amy and her good ideas. 'Listen Amy,' she said, 'if I tell you something, you're to promise that you'll never ever tell anyone else ...'

Amy listened with widening eyes as Megan told her the full story.

'But how did you get inside his body?' Amy wanted to know. 'Did you just think yourself inside him or what?'

'I don't know. It just ... well, it just happened.'

'And how did you get out again?'

Megan thought about it. There'd been a brief moment of panic when she'd towered over herself in the field and wondered how on earth she was going to get back to being Megan.

'I had awful tummy-ache afterwards,' she said, 'from all that grass.'

'You don't know, do you? Are you really really sure it happened at all?' Amy's voice was full of doubt.

'Yes, it really happened, and yes, if you must know, I'm not sure how I got into being him or got back to being me. It was quite scary.'

'Because if–' Amy's voice skidded to a stop. 'Oh, Megan,

what if Mr O'Neill does buy Jack? And what if he sends him to the glue factory like he said. It might not be Jack he sends. It might be you!'

CHAPTER 4

Four legs are wobblier than two

Megan marched up the drive to the big house. Her face was pale, but determined, as she banged on the door.

'Hello,' she said, when it opened. 'You're the old man who's selling this house to Mr O'Neill, aren't you?'

The old man laughed, though Megan didn't see anything funny. 'Yes, in a way I am. I'm seeing to the arrangements for the real owner.'

'Oh.' Megan was surprised. 'Aren't you the real owner then?'

'No. It's old Mr Garside's niece who owns the place. And she needs to sell up.'

'Well listen, I just wanted to ask you, do you have to sell to Mr O'Neill? Wouldn't someone else do?'

'Certainly someone else would do. But there's not many want these big places these days, and it's in quite a state.'

'Right then. That's good.' Megan became business-like. 'You tell Mr O'Neill that he can't have it because you're selling it to someone else.'

The old man laughed again. 'That's all well and good, young lady, but who is this someone else? Are you going to buy it yourself?'

Megan bristled at his tone. 'I might. I don't see why I shouldn't.'

'You've the money have you?'

'Well … no, but listen, you can't sell it to Mr O'Neill. What about Jack?'

'Jack?' The old man's expression softened. He opened the door wider. 'I didn't know you had an interest in Jack.' His face was serious now as he listened to what Megan had to say. 'I appreciate your concern, young lady,' he said. 'But there's not much I can do and Mr O'Neill did promise me faithfully that he'd let Jack stay on.'

The old man seemed sympathetic, but Megan didn't risk telling him the full story. Instead she said, 'If you can't find anyone else to buy the house and things, can't you find someone else to buy Jack? How much is he?'

The old man shook his head. 'It isn't a case of price, young lady, it's that no one wants an old gentleman like him. He has no pedigree to recommend him, and he does nothing but eat.'

As the old man went on, the grimness of Megan's expression softened and became a grin of delight. It was going to be all right after all. She said her goodbyes and raced home.

'Mum,' she shouted as she burst through the door. 'Mum, I've decided. I'm going to buy Jack.'

'Megan, you can't! Apart from anything else, you haven't any money.'

'That doesn't matter.' Megan's grin widened. She'd known her mother would say that. 'The old man says they just want him to go to a good home. He says they don't want paying.'

Megan waited with diminishing confidence for her mother's expression to lift. She was expecting her to smile in relief, to say, 'That's wonderful, all problems solved.' Instead she said, 'But what about food bills, and where would you keep him?'

'In the garden to start with. Just until I find him a new field.'

'Megan, just look!' Her mother pointed out through the kitchen window. 'Jack wouldn't have room to turn round and think what a mess he'd make of the tubs.'

Megan looked. A bit of her optimism leaked away. It was rather small and cramped for a whole horse.

'We'll keep him in Amy's garden then, until we find somewhere better.' Megan tried to push away from her a mental picture of the manicured lawn and flowerbeds that were Amy's parents' pride and joy. Her mother didn't bother to respond. They both knew that idea was a non-starter.

'So how is it that people like Naylor O'Neill can keep millions of ponies all over the place and I can't have a single horse?' she burst out.

'She's only got one, Megan, and she keeps it down at the stables. And before you ask. No. We couldn't possibly afford their livery charges. Jack will be fine. I don't know why you're so worried.'

The sound of the doorbell interrupted them.

'She won't let me,' Megan greeted Amy, and they both turned gloomy faces to Megan's mum.

'For heaven's sake, stop this nonsense, the pair of you. I've enough to worry about with Aunt Ellie coming to stay.'

'Aunt Ellie!' Megan stared at her mother. 'You never told me.'

'Didn't I? Well I've been so busy, I must have forgotten.'

'When's she coming?'

'She'll be arriving any minute.'

Megan and Amy looked at each other aghast, then turned and ran.

When they'd put enough distance between themselves and Megan's house, they slowed and turned dismal faces to each other.

'All this going on ...' Megan held up her hands in despair.

'And your Aunt Ellie as well,' finished Amy and then mimicked in a sing-song voice. 'It's never too early to learn how to behave. No one notices clean fingernails.'

It was a good impersonation of her aunt, but Megan was in no mood for it. 'Oh shut up, Amy. It'll be bad enough listening to her, without having to listen to you as well. What are we going to do about Jack? We've got to find someone to take him before Mr O'Neill gets his hands on him, but I don't know who. Horses cost money even when you don't have to pay for them.'

'Your Aunt Ellie wouldn't want him would she?'

'No, she said horses were germ-ridden smelly creatures last time she was here.'

'What a horrid thing to say!'

Megan kicked out at a tin can in the gutter. 'Well I agreed with her. But it was different, we were talking about Naylor O'Neill's pony. I said, yes, Naylor looks like a smelly germ when she's riding her fat pony.'

They both laughed, but then quietened as they reached the corner of the lane.

'Megan?'

'What?'

'Nothing.'

Megan stopped. 'What is it? Don't say nothing, because you wouldn't have said Megan in the first place if it'd been nothing. If you've got any good ideas, you'd better say them. We're running out of time.'

Amy hesitated, then said, 'I want to see you do it.'

'Do what?'

'Swap with Jack.'

Megan gave an uncertain laugh. She looked towards the field. Jack had his head down as usual munching away. 'I don't know if I can. It just happens.'

They went and sat on the gate. 'Go on, Megan, see if you can.'

Megan called to Jack, who strolled towards them. Why does he come so slowly when he's got all those legs, she thought? And as she urged him to hurry, they were suddenly all her legs. She fought a desperate battle to keep them from tangling, and saw alarm on Amy's face as she lurched closer. Amy was sitting on the top rung looking from one to the other of them. Megan turned to the figure of herself standing by the gate and stared into its eyes. Yes, she could see Jack. She was looking at her own body, but deep into Jack's eyes, which seemed to radiate puzzlement at her struggles with his four legs.

Then a look of alarm spread across his face and his arms began to flail. With a soft plop he sat down hard on the wet earth.

Megan laughed. 'Well, you're not much better at it than I am.'

It can't be so difficult, she thought, I did it before when I wasn't thinking about it. I bet I can. I won't try to think, I'll just do it.

'Just watch this, Amy,' she shouted and set off at breakneck speed around the edge of the field. The figures in her wide field of vision were tiny dots in no time. Panting with the exhilaration of the sprint, she skidded to a halt at the far fence.

'By heck, old boy. What's got into you lately?' came a voice from behind.

'Just having a run.' The words were out before she'd thought. If she could have done, she'd have clapped a hoof over her mouth. How would she ever explain a talking horse? But the old man didn't look at all surprised. He leant over and gave her a brisk pat on the neck and she realised that the words hadn't come out as words. They'd come out as a whinny.

From the corner of her eye she saw herself by the far gate

reaching to pull a leaf off the bush. Oh no, not another night of tummy-ache!

Shouting at the top of her voice, 'Amy! Amy! Stop him!' she hurtled across the field, leaving the old man shaking his head as he followed her progress.

'The old man was really surprised to see Jack running about,' she told Amy as they walked back. 'It was a good feeling going that fast. You know I could have just leapt right up over the gate if I'd wanted to.'

'I'm glad you didn't,' Amy said. 'No one's used to seeing him run about.'

Megan swung round. 'Amy, what if we could make Jack do something really clever. We could make someone want to buy him. It'll need both of us. You've got to stop him making me eat leaves and things. Come on, we've got things to plan.'

They hurried to Megan's house, rushed in and up the stairs, but a voice halted them. 'Megan! How nice to see you, dear. Come and introduce me to your little friend. Why, it's Amy, isn't it? I remember you, dear. How do you do? Now, girls, what have I told you about fingernails?'

CHAPTER 5

A walk with Aunt Ellie

Megan and her mother faced each other over the breakfast table the next morning.

'Megan, it's very kind of Aunt Ellie to offer to go for a walk with you.' Megan's mother turned her back on Aunt Ellie as she spoke and gave Megan a look that said, yes I know what you're thinking, but we've all got to do our bit while she's here.

'Oh all right.' Megan glared. 'But Amy's coming too and we've already arranged where we're going.'

'But I thought we might catch the bus into town, Megan dear. I might be tempted to buy you a nice new frock.' Aunt Ellie slipped an imitation flower into the buttonhole of her coat as she spoke.

Megan scowled but, catching her mother's eye, refrained from comment except to mutter, 'They're not frocks. They're dresses.' Then an inspiration struck her. 'But Aunt Ellie, we've made an appointment. It isn't good manners to miss an appointment.'

'Yes, that's true, Megan. I'm pleased to see you taking an interest in these things. Where is your appointment and with whom?'

'It's with Amy and a horse called Jack.' Hearing a sharp

intake of breath she hurried on, 'And with an old man who's lending us a saddle and things. Amy's going riding.'

'Oh I see. You've been bitten by that bug have you? Never mind, it can be a ladylike pursuit if you wear gloves.'

'I thought Amy hated riding,' her mother said, surprised.

'Yes, but she did have lessons that time, so at least she knows how.'

'Won't you be riding too? It doesn't seem fair that Amy should ride and you not. If that's what you want to do.'

'How can I–' Megan swallowed the words 'sit on my own back'. This was a very complicated business. 'Come on, Aunt Ellie, we mustn't be late.'

The old man put the saddle and bridle on Jack. He'd given them permission to take Jack to the local show next weekend, and said, 'I'm all in favour of what you're trying to do, young ladies. I'd much sooner someone else took the old lad than leave him to Mr O'Neill. Mind you, if you'd asked me a week ago I'd have said you hadn't a chance of doing anything with him, but by gum, the way I've caught him racing about this last week, maybe he'll come good for you.'

'Oh yes, he's sure to win,' Megan said, looking with some concern at the metal bar in Jack's mouth. It looked like it might hurt. And as for that strap round his middle ... 'Hey, do you have to pull as tight as that? I'll ... er ... he ... won't be able to breathe.'

'He'll be fine, won't you, lad?' The old man patted Jack's

neck. 'Though it's a good few years since you were in harness.'

Aunt Ellie stood erect and disapproving on the side lines. She may not know much about horses, her silence seemed to say, but she knew a ladylike horse when she saw one, and ladylike, Jack certainly was not.

'Up you go!' The old man hoisted Amy into the saddle and they set off into the field.

Jack stopped and put his head down to eat. Amy hauled on the reins and urged him on.

'Come on Amy, you'll have to do better than that,' shouted Megan. 'They get timed you know. He's got to go faster than anyone else. You're supposed to know how to ride.'

'You're a bit optimistic, young lady,' said the old man. Then to Amy, 'Go on, give him a kick.'

Amy obliged and Jack set off at a gentle amble. Megan jumped up and down in frustration. 'That's no good, Amy. Get him going properly!'

'Megan dear, don't jump like that. You're splashing me with mud.'

'Go on, Amy!'

'That's it.' The old man joined in. 'Show him who's boss!'

Megan, one minute fists clenched to drive them on, suddenly found herself saying 'Ooof!' as Amy's heels dug into her side.

'Don't kick me!' she shouted, bounding forward and galloping across the field. Amy's thin scream cut through the air, but Megan barely heard it. Then with an unfamiliar metallic jerk, the bar that she hadn't noticed in her mouth was making its presence felt and pulling her back. There was no pain, but surprise skidded her to a halt. She watched in amazement as Amy sailed in a graceful arc over her head and landed in a heap at the bottom of the hedge.

The old man was full of apologies. 'I've never seen him do that, not even when we were first breaking him.'

Aunt Ellie obviously thought it was time to call it a day. 'Megan dear, I think that's enough. And you should show a little concern for your friend. She's taken quite a tumble.'

Megan watched aghast as her figure looked up at Aunt Ellie with Jack's eyes, gave her a benevolent smile, then reached forward and plucked the flowers from her buttonhole with its mouth.

Before Aunt Ellie could react, Amy, covered in mud from head to toe stormed furiously up and shouted into Megan's face. Megan from her vantage point above them all, watched Amy storm between Jack and a spluttering Aunt Ellie, and saw that, cross though she was, Amy was continuing to play her part. She was standing in front of Megan's body, but her eyes and her shouts were all aimed at the real Megan inside Jack.

'I can't understand a word you're saying,' Amy screeched, 'so how am I supposed to know what you're going to do next?'

'Sorry,' said Megan, and heard the gentle whicker escape Jack's lips.

'Why, I do believe he's saying he's sorry,' said the old man.

'Humph!' said Amy, snatching Aunt Ellie's imitation

flower from Megan's lips and throwing it to the ground. 'And STOP eating things.'

After a lot of pleading and apologetic snorts from Megan, Amy said she'd have, 'One more try, but any funny business, and that's it!'

She was very reluctant to try a small jump, though Megan urged her with frantic whinnies. It was so important. They would have to jump round a whole course and faster than anyone else, so they must practice.

'All right,' Amy said. 'That small log. The LOW end.'

They got over it in one piece, but could see from Aunt Ellie's face that they would get no points for ladylike grace.

'It's a lot harder than I thought, having to balance you as well,' she neighed, thinking it was a good thing she hadn't tried the big fence like she'd planned, just to show Amy how easy it would be.

'How long will you be, Amy?' Aunt Ellie's voice sounded pained. This hadn't been what she'd had in mind when she suggested a walk.

'I'll say nothing in front of strangers dear,' she added, in a stern aside to Megan. 'But your behaviour has been quite bizarre and I intend to let your mother know. Just because you didn't get a turn is no reason to loll about over the gate making such peculiar noises.'

'Swap now, Megan. Quick!' Amy hissed.

Megan looked down at them. She stared hard at her body, willing herself to slip back into it. Nothing happened. She tried to fight a rising panic. What if she was stuck?

Then she gave a great sigh of relief as the peculiar taste of imitation flowers filled her mouth, and the disapproving gaze of Aunt Ellie appeared in front of her.

Her whispered discussion with Amy was not a cheerful one. It had been much harder than Megan expected, having Amy on her back.

'I could do it on my own easily.'

They checked with the old man. No, he said, he'd never heard of a competition where the horse went round on its own.

Amy said, 'It's not that I'm scared or anything, but let's not practice again until Saturday.'

Megan sighed. Amy didn't really want to try again ever, and she could sympathise. A part of her wanted to walk away from Jack and never come back, but it was no good.

Every day brought Jack closer to the knacker's yard and only she and Amy could save him.

CHAPTER 6

The show

The day of the show dawned bright and sunny. They walked down the road with Jack between them.

'Shouldn't you swap with him, Megan?'

'I'll wait till we get there.' Megan was uneasy. Far from having to fight to stay inside her own body, as she thought she'd have to, she hadn't been able to feel Jack's mind at all. Maybe it's because I'm nervous, she thought. Or maybe it's Amy being nervous who's putting me off – for Amy was white-faced at the thought of trying to ride Jack in front of all those people.

'It'll be all right,' Megan said. 'I'll get round faster than any of them ...' If only I can swap, she added silently.

They ignored the derisive jeers of Naylor O'Neill and her gang as they entered the show-ground.

'Tie yourself to that post,' Amy told Megan, 'and swap!'

Megan took her time looping her belt through the post.

'Go and line up with the others,' she said. 'Go on. It'll be okay once you get in there.'

Megan watched with interest as a succession of ponies entered the ring and raced round scattering the poles. Her anxiety lifted. This was going to be easy. She caught Amy's eye and gave her an encouraging smile. It wasn't going to matter about going fast. All she needed to do was leave the fences up.

Megan gritted her teeth as Amy and Jack made their way at snail's pace into the ring.

'Are you ready?' the woman in charge shouted doubtfully to Amy.

Amy nodded and the woman rang the bell for them to start.

Jack's head dropped to the ground and he nipped off a tuft of grass. Amy hauled hard at the reins and kicked at Jack's sides. He took a step forward then stretched up his head and yawned.

Naylor O'Neill and her cronies fell about in paroxysms of helpless mirth.

Megan clenched and unclenched her fists and raged.

Amy, in a flurry of hand flapping, urgings and kicks that should have won her a Grand National at least, got Jack to stroll up to the first obstacle, a red and white pole balanced twenty centimetres above the ground. Jack looked down at it as though not sure what Amy expected of him, then he stepped his front feet over it one at a time and stopped.

Amy flapped and kicked. Naylor's gang were helpless and even the woman with the bell was smiling.

Then all of a sudden Megan felt Amy's heels in her side.

'Hold on, Amy!' she shouted in a great whinny and bounded forward.

Now she'd show them. Careless of Amy's desperate entreaties to 'be careful, Megan' she dashed from obstacle to obstacle, springing into the air when they seemed to be underfoot. These piddling little sticks that she could hardly see below her big brown nose were so awkward. Things kept getting under her feet and tipping her off balance. But she scrambled her way round. She would show them! They were at the final line now. Three little obstacles to go. She caught sight of Naylor O'Neill's face. It was a mixture of uncertain laughter, amazement and disbelief. Naylor of course had never seen Jack go at this speed before.

Oh no, she was seeing Naylor through her own eyes. She was slipping away from Jack. GO ON JACK, she thought wildly. She'd given him a good start, just one straight line of little fences to go.

Megan could feel he was doing his best. He wasn't sure why, but this was what they wanted him to do, so he did it. He mustered himself to a steady rolling gait and lumbered down the line, a look of earnest concentration on his face. Above him, expression blank with dismay, clung Amy. Jack never once broke stride. Coloured poles and imitation bricks flew around him like confetti as he ploughed through the small obstacles.

A huge wave of disappointment burst over Megan. After all her hard work, why couldn't Jack just have copied what she had done …?

Her train of thought lurched to a halt. Her eyes took in the wider picture. The whole ring looked as though a lorry load of coloured poles had been tipped in from a height. Not a single obstacle after the first remained intact. She'd flattened the lot. Jack had done his best after all. He had copied what she'd done.

Amy, her face burning with mortification, hustled Jack out of the ring as fast as she could make him go. They left to a great burst of applause and laughter.

'That's young Amy Atkinson, isn't it?' said a voice behind Megan. She turned to see a man making his way towards her, walking awkwardly with a stick. He might be someone's brother, or maybe dad. He looked vaguely familiar.

She gave him a curt nod. 'And there's no need to laugh at them. They'd have won if they hadn't knocked them all down.' Then feeling the need to mount some sort of attack on him because he seemed to be laughing at Amy, 'Why have you got a walking stick? You're not old.'

'An accident with a recalcitrant animal,' said the stranger, still smiling. 'It'll be okay eventually. Anyway, they did fine. He's quite an age isn't he, that old pony she was riding?'

'Yes, he's quite old, but,' Megan went on with sudden hope, 'he's still good enough for someone to buy him. He only isn't very good at those small fences because he can't see them. His nose is too big. He can do hedges and big things. He's for sale if you're interested. In fact you won't even have to pay if you give him a good home.'

The man was looking at Jack, now being dragged along by Amy who had dismounted.

'What did he do in his younger days?' the man asked.

'He pulled the farm cart.' The old man had told them all about it.

'I don't suppose he had much call to jump fences when he was pulling a cart.'

'No, I suppose not,' said Megan, who hadn't given the matter any thought before.

'I think that's why he's not very good at it. He doesn't know how. Mind you,' he stopped smiling and looked puzzled. 'He put on quite a turn of speed. She must have stuck a pin in him.'

'Amy wouldn't do that!' Megan was indignant.

'If you say so.' The man gave her a nod, turned and limped off.

Amy didn't spare a glance for the stranger as she stormed up, pulling Jack behind her. 'I want us to go home right now,' she said.

'But Amy, what about waiting to see if anyone wants to buy Jack?'

'You stay then!' And she threw the reins at Megan and flounced off.

It was typical of the whole disastrous day that Megan, as she wended her way home, found herself without warning, on four legs again. Jack himself was tired and kept lolling Megan's body up against hedges or trying to snatch at any greenery that came within reach. Megan had to grasp a mouthful of her own jacket and push herself along the road.

A car drove past in a burst of derision yelled from the back windows. It was Naylor and her cronies. Megan, plodding her way along, pushing her own comatose form, wasn't even able to stick out her tongue at them.

35

CHAPTER 7

The big house at dusk

It was a couple of days after the show. Megan slouched along the road in the encroaching dusk. She was going past the big house, but round the front to avoid Jack's field. She didn't want to go home. Aunt Ellie was threatening to take her out, Amy wasn't speaking to her, and she couldn't even go and talk to the old man because he was away for a few days. At least there was no chance of bumping into creepy Mr O'Neill because he was away too.

She kicked out at a stone, and looked up as she heard the sound of a car engine. It would be just her luck to kick a stone at a car by accident and get blamed. The car swung in through the gates of the big house.

Megan gasped. That had been Nathan O'Neill's car.

But Naylor had distinctly said that her uncle was away.

Megan crept round the side of the gatepost and started up the drive. To her horror, she found herself bathed in the bright white of the security lights. She ducked back against the wall, panting with the scare, but at the same time felt a tingle of exhilaration. In that brief flash of light, she'd caught the gleam of painted chrome. Two cars were tucked away by the outhouses. And one of them was Nathan

O'Neill's. Why would anyone park there when the old man was away, unless they didn't want to be seen?

A part of her wanted to pull out her phone and ring the police, tell them to come at once and take Naylor's uncle to jail, but she'd probably get into trouble. She could ring her mum, who might say it was okay to tell the police, but nah, her mum would just tell her to come home and talk to Aunt Ellie.

She just had to know what he was up to. There was no way to get close from here but if she went to the other side and crept across Jack's field, she might spot Nathan O'Neill through the hedge.

Jack was dozing in a corner and Megan tried hard not to look at him, not even to think about him, as she surveyed the lie of the land. Yes, she could get across the field, but then she'd have to cross the garden. If they spotted her, she'd have to run and they'd catch her easily. She shuddered at the thought.

'Hey!' She jumped with sudden fright.

A large furry nose pushed its way into her pocket. Jack had wandered over to say hello. 'Oh go away. Can't you think of anything except eating? If you had any sense, you'd get across there and see what that man's up to.'

Of course! She couldn't go wandering about the grounds of the big house, but Jack could.

This time, she was barely conscious of the transition. She was speeding across the field in great bounding strides. There was no sign of anyone about so, taking a deep breath and measuring the distance with her eye, she sprang into the air as she neared the far fence, sailed over and on to the lawn beyond. Hedges were easy. Big enough to see.

The springy turf felt good underfoot. Soft and cool. Her hooves sank right in.

And there he was. She could see the unmistakable outline of Nathan O'Neill inside the house. He was talking to someone in the big dining room. Who could it be? The old man was the only person who lived here.

She crept closer. Gravel crunched underfoot as she crossed a small path. She held her breath, but the figures inside the house never faltered, so it couldn't have been as loud as she'd thought. If she could sneak up the steps past the big stone pots and on to the terrace, she'd be close enough to peep in through the big French window.

The stone steps were wide and shallow. They would be no problem to someone as proficient as she in equine locomotion. I'm better at it than Jack, she thought. He's never jumped that hedge in his life. But it wasn't until she'd started up that she realised just what a serious obstacle these shallow steps were. She couldn't see a single one of the four legs she was trying to control. The stone was smooth and slippery, her hooves kept shooting off at odd angles until she could hardly tell what direction she was pointing in, or if she was going up or down.

Both back legs slid off to one side. Oh no, this would be a ducking in the ornamental fishpond for sure. Then her rear end crashed to a bone-crunching stop against something which wobbled and then fell. From the corner of her eye she saw one of the huge stone pots tumble into the water with an enormous bang and splash.

The echoes died down as she fought to stay upright. The top of the terrace was like an ice rink. She slid helpless until a bump brought her to a sudden halt. Her nose was pressed tight against the big window. She was eyeball to eyeball with the most alarmed face she'd ever seen. It wasn't Nathan O'Neill. It was a stranger.

'It's okay, Mr O'Neill,' she heard a shaky voice say. 'It's just a horse.'

'A horse!' roared O'Neill leaping up from behind a settee where he'd been crouching. Megan thought she'd never seen such a red face since she'd outwitted Naylor at games. And she could see the same O'Neill rage as he struggled to open the French window. She heard a bellow of fury followed by, '... is there a gun anywhere ...?'

Slipping and sliding over the smooth surface, nearly upending herself in an involuntary rush down the steps, she fled, ploughing her way across the lawn, feeling her hooves dig in deep, as great lumps of turf flew in her wake. And with the last of her energy, she threw herself at the hedge and crashed into the field in a welter of broken branches and twigs, and staggered across to lean panting at the gate.

No one followed. Safe for now.

But it can't be good for Jack, she thought, all this running about at his age. And oh no, it wasn't going to be good for her either. While she'd been fighting stone pots, Jack had been at the hawthorn hedge.

By the end of school the next day the hawthorn tummy-ache had just about worn off. Megan felt hungry and mean. She would have confronted Naylor earlier if she'd felt up to it. Now she did. As the crowd split into school-bussers and walk-homers, she pushed in front of Naylor and said, 'Your uncle's up to no good at the big house.'

Megan expected denial, but Naylor surprised her with a sly smile.

'Yeah well, what if he is? You're not going to stop him. Ha Ha Ha!'

Naylor began to dance round Megan, prodding her with a ruler.

'Get off. Stop doing that!'

Megan snatched out, but Naylor side-stepped and continued her taunting.

'Come and look at stupid Megan Crewe,' she chanted as more of their classmates drew near to see what was going on.

'Just you stop that, Naylor O'Neill,' Megan shouted furiously. 'You're as bad as that creepy uncle of yours.'

'And you're as bad as your batty Aunt Ellie,' called one of Naylor's sycophants.

Megan coloured up. She'd hoped Aunt Ellie's visit had gone unnoticed.

'Come on now, you lot. What's going on?' At the sound of an adult voice, the tormentors drew back.

'I'm just telling everyone to line up for the bus, Mr Connor,' said Naylor, adding, 'and Megan Crewe's not behaving.'

'Come on, get yourselves in line. The bus is here.' The order was aimed at them all and caused Naylor to scowl. Megan smirked. Mr Connor didn't like people telling tales.

Naylor vented her annoyance on Amy. 'You can sit at the front where I can keep an eye on you,' she ordered and Amy slunk off down the bus.

Megan, who had learnt a thing or two in the weeks that Naylor had been bus monitor said loudly, 'She's not making me sit at the front. I'm going at the back.'

'You get down the front, Megan Crewe, or you're for it. I'm in charge.'

Megan went to sit with Amy, who was still being a bit cold, but who thawed a little at Megan deliberately joining her in the least favoured seats. Before either of them could speak, they were surprised to hear Naylor's voice saying, 'And you get down there too, Judith. If you go taking sides with wimps, you can go and sit with them.'

Megan and Amy exchanged a glance and moved up as Judith, one of Naylor's special friends, squeezed into the seat beside them.

'What have you done to Naylor?' Megan asked in a low voice.

Judith gave her a sharp look then with a cautious glance over her shoulder whispered, 'I said it was wrong what her uncle Nathan was up to while that old man's away. He's got no right. It's cruel.'

'But what is he up to?'

'I thought you knew. That's why you were having a go at Naylor, isn't it?'

'No, I just knew he was up to something. I didn't know what. Why, what is it?'

'It's that horse. That one that you and Amy are trying to save. He's got the vet coming tonight while the old man's still away. He's going to have it put down.'

'But ... but ...' Amy was speechless.

'He can't,' Megan burst out. 'It's against the law ... isn't it?'

'I don't know,' said Judith. 'Naylor said it'd broken through its hedge and done some damage and it was the best thing for it.'

'Megan,' hissed Amy. 'The old man. Ring him.'

'It's no good. It'll just be the answer machine at the big house.' Megan pulled out her phone anyway and punched in the number. Doing something was better than doing nothing. A mechanical voice spoke in her ear.

'Told you,' she said.

'Leave a voicemail,' Amy urged. 'He might call in to get his messages, to see if anything's happened while he's away.'

'Mr O'Neill's having Jack put down by a vet while you're away. You've got to come back quick or get the police to lock him up or something.' That should be clear enough but Megan wasn't reassured. Grown-ups always got the wrong idea about things and wasted time.

'It's no good, Amy,' she said. 'We're going to have to do something ourselves.'

CHAPTER 8

An Encounter with Aunt Ellie

Aunt Ellie was insufferable.

When Megan had first burst in, with Amy close on her heels, she'd been pleased to learn that her parents were out at the garden centre. Aunt Ellie, knew nothing about homework schedules. They would be able to rush straight out and round to Jack's field. At least, that's what they'd thought.

'Certainly not, girls! You can't go anywhere without having your tea. I've made chicken pie.'

They were washed and at the table in record time. As soon as their plates arrived, they fell upon them, choking the hot food down, deaf to entreaties not to 'eat like savages'.

Megan finished first and leapt to her feet, only to subside again at Aunt Ellie's stern command. 'Stay in your seat, Megan, until everyone has finished.' Megan clenched her fists and glared at Amy, who shovelled vegetables and pastry into her mouth until her cheeks ballooned like a gerbil gathering peanuts. As soon as Amy crashed her knife and fork to the plate, they pushed back their chairs, only to be halted once again. 'I won't tell you again girls! You wait until everyone has finished before you leave the table. And I am still eating.'

'But my mum lets me,' Megan cried in frustration.

'While your parents are out, Megan, it is up to me to see that you behave properly.'

Megan exchanged an agonised look with Amy as they followed each forkful from Aunt Ellie's plate to her mouth. Then Megan had an inspiration, 'Aunt Ellie? Er ... can I have some more pie? It was really nice. I thought I'd had enough, but I think I could fit some more in.' Again, she pushed her chair back, preparatory to rising, 'I can get it out of the oven myself.'

'No no, dear. You sit down. I'll get it.'

Amy glared at her scandalised. 'What about Jack?' she mouthed as Aunt Ellie left the room.

'I dropped a pie dish once,' Megan whispered, 'I knew she'd go and get it herself. Listen.' There was a click from the kitchen. 'That's the oven door. Come on, quick, while she's got that hot dish in her hands and she can't chase us.'

Amy looked horrified, but Megan knew she wouldn't stay behind on her own to face Aunt Ellie. They raced for the front door and freedom.

'You're really going to catch it,' Amy said, when they'd stopped running. 'You'd better turn your phone off.'

'Turn yours off too.'

'I don't need to. I forgot it.'

'I hope we're not too late, Amy.'

When they reached the field, Megan heaved a sigh of relief. Jack was there, eating as usual. 'Whew! Now we've got to decide what to do.'

'Oh Megan, look!'

Megan swung round. There in the distance was Nathan O'Neill with a big man carrying a bag. That must be the vet.

'What can we do?' wailed Megan. 'Where can we take him?'

There was only one thing for it. 'Listen Amy,' she said urgently. 'You've got to make sure we stay together and ...' She stopped, desperately trying to put her thoughts into order. Where could they go?

Anywhere, she thought. Anywhere is better than here, just for now. 'Listen Amy, I'm not sure where we're going to go, but just remember Jack can't do doors and things. You'll have to help.'

'What do you ...?' Amy might have finished the question, but Megan didn't hear it. She was seeing Amy from a different, wider angle. The gate was between them, but it wouldn't be for long. Megan saw her friend turn in alarm, saw her catch hold of the sleeve of the now blank-eyed figure next to her. Thank goodness, she's caught on, thought Megan as she sailed over the gate and skidded to a stop. Had O'Neill seen them? No, he was still talking to the vet over by the big house. He hadn't noticed.

Megan, striding out on Jack's four legs, led the way. Amy followed, dragging an uncomplaining Jack by the belt.

'Megan.' Amy panted along after her. 'You can't go back to your house.'

Megan tried to send a thought at Jack, but his mind seemed half asleep. So she just whinnied and marched on.

After a moment, Amy said, 'Your garden shed?'

Megan nodded Jack's big head up and down.

'Okay, I see what you mean about doors now.' Amy was silent for a while as she dragged Jack along after the speeding Megan. Then she panted out, 'Only we'll have to think of something else pretty quick. Your mum and dad will be putting all their garden stuff in there. Megan, why do they …?'

Megan gritted Jack's teeth as Amy asked the question she always asked when the garden centre came up. Why did Megan's mum and dad spend so much time and money at the garden centre when they had so little room? Megan, who'd never been very interested in her parents' horticultural interests, sometimes attempted a reply about special plants and tubs. On this occasion, she simply gave an impatient snort. How Amy expected her to talk about complicated plant matters at a time like this, and with Jack's voice box, she couldn't imagine!

'I suppose it'll do for now.' Amy's thoughts had obviously returned to the shed. 'But wait a minute.' Megan felt a tug on her tail. 'Let me go first to see if it's safe.'

Megan watched as Amy, hauling Jack by the belt, crept towards the gate. She beckoned and Megan clip-clopped up to join her. There was no one in sight as they entered the front yard, but then Megan stopped and stared at Amy in dismay. Voices from the garden. Her mum and dad were back already.

Megan started to turn the awkward bulk of Jack's body in the small space, when Amy stopped her with a horrified stare and upraised hand.

'Girls! Girls! Is that you?'

Aunt Ellie who must have been out searching for them was hurrying down the pavement. She would be upon them in no time.

Giving Amy a great boost from behind with her huge nose, Megan pushed her at the front door. They barged through it together and Megan found herself wedged in the tiny hallway. There was only one thing to do. Amy needed no more pushing. She scrambled up the stairs and swung Megan's bedroom door wide.

Megan, seeing the way clear, hurled herself at the narrow staircase feeling an overabundance of legs churning beneath her as she fought to climb up. She panted and gasped and scrambled and at last, with a great lunge fell face first into her bedroom. There was no time to get her breath. Scrabbling to her feet, she turned with difficulty and, pushing the door almost shut with her nose, put an eye to the crack. Amy was racing down again.

Aunt Ellie was in the hallway, taking off her scarf. 'Don't clatter down the stairs, dear,' she admonished. Then, 'Megan!' in horrified tones.

Megan stared wildly through the narrow crack. She saw herself standing in the hallway, three long fronds from her mother's Christmas cactus hanging from her mouth. She saw Amy snatch them out and drag her by the belt back up the stairs. She saw Aunt Ellie, face like thunder, purse her lips and head off to hang up her coat.

The two figures crashed into the bedroom and Amy slumped down on the bed.

'Oh Megan this is awful. What are we going to do?'

Megan pushed Amy off the bed and towards the window. She didn't bother with Jack's minimal powers as a translator. Amy would understand.

'They're both in the garden. They're putting things in the shed.'

Right then, thought Megan. We just need Aunt Ellie out of the way.

Fortunately, Amy's brain was working at double-quick speed. 'If I get her in the kitchen ...' she began, and reached for the door handle.

But it turned on its own before she could touch it.

'Now girls, I need to have a very strong word about—'

Aunt Ellie marched in and stopped with a great gasp.

For one long moment, they stood frozen, the figures of Amy and Megan to one side, Aunt Ellie face to face with Jack's big brown nose.

Oh no, thought Megan, now we're really for it.

Seconds passed. Aunt Ellie didn't move. Her mouth hung open.

Amy stared horror-struck. Megan gulped. No one in the history of the entire world, she was sure, had ever been caught with a horse in their bedroom.

Megan caught Amy's eye. The slight movement of the big

brown head rooted Aunt Ellie even more firmly to the spot, but it roused Amy to action.

Grabbing Megan's belt she dragged Jack out on to the landing and down the stairs. Megan from inside Jack's all-seeing eye caught the movement of the front door as Amy pulled it wide.

In one bound she was past Aunt Ellie and hurtling down. And once she'd started, there was no going back. Her four legs became forty, each having a desperate scramble to beat her nose to the bottom of the flight.

She didn't have time to think about it, but her wide vision seemed to tell her that Aunt Ellie hadn't moved a muscle.

Her front hooves reached the hall floor a fraction ahead of her nose and the momentum shot her out of the door and down the path.

Amy had the gate held wide and in no time the three of them were fleeing as fast as their four pairs of legs would carry them.

CHAPTER 9

Cousin Tony

They crept towards the field, Megan keeping to the grass verge to muffle the tell-tale sound of hoof beats. She'd tried taking a turn towards Amy's house, but Amy said 'No!' in such a firm voice that Megan had turned away.

'We'll go to the big house,' Amy said. 'Round the front. We'll hide Jack in one of the sheds until the old man gets back.'

It wasn't a bad plan, as long as they could sneak past O'Neill and the vet who would be out looking for them.

As they got nearer, Megan stopped and pressed Jack's body into the hedge. Amy crept forward then she stood up straight with a big smile, and beckoned to Megan.

'He's back,' she called.

They stood and watched. There, at the far side of the field, stood the old man, his voice raised angrily at O'Neill and the vet. The vet turned to O'Neill and his words floated over to them, 'You gave me to understand, Mr O'Neill …'

O'Neill shrugged, but there was fury in every line of his body. Megan and Amy heard the words, '… another few days …'

They knew what he was saying. Another few days and he could do as he liked with Jack.

'Quick Megan,' Amy hissed. 'Jump over the gate.'

'I can't,' said Megan, with surprise. 'I've turned back.'

They looked at each other, and Amy let her hand drop from Megan's belt. Jack, inside his own body again, wandered to the other side of the lane where the grass was longer. Megan looked at the padlock on the gate. 'How are we going to get him in?'

'Well done, young ladies, well done.'

The old man hurried towards them. 'I rushed back as soon as I got your message,' he said. 'I don't know how you got him out, but thank goodness you did. You were right.' He turned to Megan. 'Everything you said about him.' He jerked his thumb in O'Neill's direction.

The old man took a key from his pocket and called to Jack who plodded across the road. 'You've saved him for today but it'll do no good in the end. He's going to have him put down the minute the place is his.'

'But now you believe us, you can tell the owner and stop her selling to Mr O'Neill. If she doesn't believe you, she can ask the vet too.'

The old man shook his head. 'He's talked the vet round. Told him it was a mistake. And anyway, no one cares too much about an old man like Jack.' He turned to the elderly horse. 'You're puffing and blowing a bit, old lad. You're as bad as me when I've been rushing up and down stairs.'

Megan and Amy avoided his eye.

They shuffled towards home, dragging their feet. The old man promised to try to get the owner to rethink, but he wasn't optimistic.

'I'll be grounded,' said Megan. 'For at least a week.'

'D'you think I'll get grounded too?'

'Oh yes. Aunt Ellie'll have told my mum, and she'll have rung your mum. I bet they're all out looking for us right now.'

'A week …' Amy's voice tailed off. Megan knew what she was thinking. In a week, it would all be over for Jack.

'What did you say about someone coming to stay?' Megan turned the conversation. The subject of Jack was too painful.

'My cousin Tony. The one from Australia. The one we thought we could send Jack to. He's moving back over here. That's why they had to sell all their animals.'

'I don't suppose …' Megan began.

'No,' said Amy. 'He hasn't even got a house yet.'

'But what about him buying the big house. Then he'd get Jack and we could sort something out afterwards if he didn't want to keep him.'

'Well …'

'I know!' Megan stopped. 'Why don't I come to your house now, and we can ask him?'

'He might be out. And what about your mum and dad?'

'I'll ring up from yours. I'll say I forgot to charge my phone. Then I can get my first telling off from a long way away. That's a good idea even if your cousin isn't there.'

In trepidation, they entered Amy's house.

'Is that you, Amy?' a voice called.

They went through and stood in the kitchen doorway, waiting for the blow to fall.

'What are you two looking so shifty about?'

'Er ... nothing ...' Obviously Megan's mum hadn't called yet.

'Does your mother know you're here, Megan?'

'Er ... no ... my phone's not charged.'

'Well don't just stand there like lemons. Go and give her a ring.'

Megan cringed as she heard her mother's voice. 'Hi Mum. I'm at Amy's. My battery's run out.'

'Okay dear. Don't be late back.'

'Right. Er ... is that all?'

'What do you mean?'

'Where's Aunt Ellie?'

'She's lying down. She said she had one of her headaches coming on. I hope you haven't been giving her grief, Megan.'

'Oh no, Mum. Course not.'

She and Amy exchanged glances as Megan put down the phone. 'Maybe Aunt Ellie's really gone batty,' whispered Megan.

'Cousin Tony's watching telly. Shall we go and talk to him about the big house?'

Megan went through behind Amy and said a gruff, 'Hello,' before she had a proper look at the man sitting on the settee. Her mouth dropped open.

'We were wondering if you wanted to buy a house near here,' Amy said. 'There's one for sale and it's got a horse with it.'

Instead of answering Amy, Cousin Tony said, 'If this is going to be a serious discussion, I need sustenance. Run upstairs and get those chocolates from my room.'

'Can I have some?' Amy said.

Her cousin swatted at her with a rolled-up newspaper. 'Be off with you, disrespectful girl. I might let you have a sliver.'

Amy grinned. 'And Megan?'

'Yes, and Megan. Now go on!'

As soon as Amy left the room, Megan turned on the man. 'You're the man at the show,' she accused him. 'You're the one who laughed at Jack.'

CHAPTER 10

Unfamiliar chocolate

Amy's cousin had a sparkly look in his eye. 'Guilty as charged,' he said, holding up his hands. 'I'm the man at the show, but don't worry, I haven't let on I was there. I've pretended absolute indifference to all mention of the nag.'

'But why?'

'Oh, don't get me wrong. I think she did extraordinarily well, to say that she was taking an elderly cart-horse on his first excursion into a show-jumping ring. But I had the impression she didn't feel she'd shown herself in the best light, so I thought it politic to deny all knowledge or interest.'

Megan digested this. 'So does that mean that you do want to have Jack or you don't?'

'I'd have no objection to giving him a home. I don't suppose he costs much to run. But I can hardly offer to house him until I've sorted out a place of my own.'

'And are you getting busy buying somewhere? There isn't much time.'

'I've seen a couple of places. I might have something sorted out in a month or so.'

'A month or so! Can't you get Jack anyway, just to be going on with?'

'Ah, but Amy implied that whoever buys the old chap must take him away, out of the clutches of the foul-hearted MacSteel.'

'O'Neill,' corrected Megan, giving Amy's cousin a black look. He wasn't taking this seriously. 'But couldn't you buy him anyway? He doesn't take up much room, and you'd soon get a new field.'

'And where would I keep him in the meantime? In my bedroom?'

Cousin Tony laughed, but Megan felt herself colour up and avoided his eye.

'Or you could just buy the house where he is already,' she said. 'It's a good one.'

'Okay,' he said, as Amy crashed back in brandishing a box of chocolates. 'I see no reason not to look the place over. How about you take me there tomorrow?'

We'll tell him all about Jack, thought Megan, while we have his chocolates. She was disappointed to see that they were chocolates in a box. Megan didn't approve of chocolates in a box. They cost loads and there was always more box than chocolate. The colour looked disappointing too. It was lighter than real chocolate. The colour of cheap buttons. Real proper chocolate like Dairy Milk or Yorkie was fat and dark and smooth all through.

Megan reached for the proffered box. The shapes were unfamiliar. She was an adept at avoiding the marzipan or the coconut or – bleugh – the Turkish Delight, but you couldn't tell with these. And yet now she looked closely, they all seemed whipped and creamy, as if the taste might be something special. After a moment's hesitation, she went for the biggest and put it in her mouth.

It made both cheeks bulge at once, but as soon as her teeth hit the surface, she knew she'd picked well. It was chocolate. Real chocolate, softer and smoother than Dairy Milk. It was like letting a whole piece melt on your tongue without that agonising wait where you had to force yourself not to bite into it. This chocolate was already soft and melty. And the taste was better than anything she'd had before.

She saw Amy with the second largest, taking a small bite into the edge. Amy was always scared of getting the Mont-thingy. One of her teeth had snapped off once when she'd bitten into a Mont-thingy, thinking it was a strawberry cream. The tooth had been loose for a week, so Megan never understood all the fuss, but Amy was wary of boxed chocolates now.

'It won't bite you,' Cousin Tony said, watching his niece's tentative assault on the chocolatey surface.

'She worried her teeth'll drop out,' explained Megan indistinctly through a mouthful of chocolatey goo.

'They'll be fine. Chocolates are okay if you clean your teeth.'

'No.' Megan wrestled the magical mouthful into submission, so she could speak. 'It's in case her teeth just drop straight out. If it's the Mont-thingy.'

Amy's cousin looked at her. 'I fear the modern child has lost the art of communication during my sojourn in sunnier climes.'

I wish he'd talk sense, thought Megan. Maybe it's all those years in Australia. She bit again through the melting mouthful and sucked the chocolate through her teeth. There'd been something different in the centre, but it had tasted like chocolate too. Chocolates filled with chocolate. What a good idea. She hoped it would catch on. 'These are mega-inpiffalicacious,' she said. 'What sort are they?'

'They're just common-or-garden Belgian chocolates. I bought them on the way over. What did you say they were?'

'Mega ... something. I made it up. It's a pity they're so small.'

'Mmmph,' agreed Amy, trying to look as though she'd finished hers too.

'You'd better have another.' Cousin Tony knew how to take a hint. 'In fact, we'd better finish the whole box. No point leaving boxes of chocolates half finished, I always say.'

Megan's eyes gleamed. Amy's cousin was more sensible than she'd realised. Maybe everything would be okay after all.

'So we'll go and have a look tomorrow then, shall we?' he said.

'Look at what?' This one was amazing. It was different from the last. Different on the outside and the inside, but it was still all chocolate. She savoured it on her tongue and then chewed and swallowed it. With Amy nibbling at the edges and her cousin still on his first, she'd get half the box to herself if she was quick.

'At that house you want me to buy.'

58

'Oh yeah, that. The old man won't mind. He'll show you the inside if you want to see it.'

'I'm not too fussy. Still, I guess it would be nice to see inside the place if I'm going to be living there. I can check to see if the roof leaks and all those boring sorts of things.'

'Oh yes, it's like a waterfall in bad weather,' said Megan, quoting the old man. 'He says it's rough on his rheumatism, but you'll be all right.'

Amy pointed to the chocolates. 'Hey, don't let him near these when you've swapped. He'll get awful tummy-ache.' Megan saw her freeze as soon as the words were out. They exchanged an agonised glance.

Cousin Tony looked from one to the other of them. 'Who's swapping what?' he said.

'Er ... the old man ... He likes chocolates too. Only he doesn't ...' Megan floundered for a convincing ending to the sentence and Amy leapt in with, 'He doesn't let Jack have them, because Jack ... Jack doesn't like ... Turkish delight ...'

'And once he snapped a tooth,' Megan improvised.

Cousin Tony looked at them through narrowed eyes. 'We'd better skip the chocolates then, when we go round. We wouldn't want everyone laid up. I'd no idea Belgian chocolates could cause such trouble.'

Nor me, thought Megan. She didn't even blame Amy for her slip, because she could have done it herself, lulled by the magical creamy blobs. That taste! Yes, Belgian chocolates might be the best ever, but they made you not very careful about what you said.

CHAPTER 11

Checking out the big house

Everything was arranged with the old man. 'Come as early as you can,' he said. 'Before O'Neill gets here.'

Megan arrived at Amy's before they'd finished breakfast, and jigged about impatiently until they were ready.

Amy's mum started to explain the quick way to the big house. Megan glared at her as she tried to hustle Amy and Cousin Tony out of the door. As if they didn't already know the way!

'Cut down the side of the field where that old pony is.'

That's easy for you to say, she thought, you don't turn into a horse every time you go past.

At the corner at the end of the road Megan tensed. Would Cousin Tony notice they weren't going the way Amy's mum had said? He didn't. He just said, 'I know I'm fresh back from the Antipodes, and might be expected to be hazy on my norths and souths, but I'm rock solid on my lefts and rights. Still, I'm sure you know best.'

Megan gave him an encouraging smile and hoped the old man would be able to understand him.

She turned to Amy. 'I might have to go the long way round forever.'

'Not if Naylor's uncle buys Jack, you won't.'

'Erk.' Megan shuddered. 'Don't even think about it. It makes shivers go up my spine. Anyway, shut up,' she ended, seeing the quizzical look Cousin Tony was giving them.

'Hmm,' he said. 'The long way round … shivers down the spine … I wonder if this could have anything to do with swapping?'

Amy gasped, but Megan, remembering the slip they'd made the day before, thought, he doesn't really know, he's just guessing. She hoped Amy wouldn't blurt anything out.

When neither of them spoke, Cousin Tony said cryptically, 'I'll bide my time. Further confectionery can always be brought to bear to loosen tongues.'

They slowed their pace as they approached the drive. It was still early, but you never knew with O'Neill.

'What are you doing?' Cousin Tony said as they crept towards the driveway. 'I don't consider this mission any kind of clandestine venture. I'm going to take a look-see at a property openly on the market, and I have every intention of behaving as though the whole business is above board. In fact I intend to walk to the door and knock. If you two wish to creep through the shrubbery and effect illicit entry like petty crooks, that's fine, but don't expect me to follow.'

Megan glared at him. 'We're checking there's no one here,' she hissed.

'Ah ha! You mean the foul-hearted MacSteel. Fear not, young maidens, I'll vanquish him with my trusty sabre.'

'It's only metal. It hasn't even got a blade.' Megan looked with disdain at the walking stick he was brandishing, adding for good measure, 'It takes seven years to grow a proper walking stick.' She'd got that from Aunt Ellie. 'And anyway, it's O'Neill, not MacSteel.'

There was one car in the drive, but it wasn't O'Neill's. They watched Cousin Tony walk up to the door and saw the old man let him in. 'Let's wait on the road,' Amy said, 'in case Naylor's uncle turns up.'

'Whose is that car?' Megan asked. 'I've seen it before.'

Amy shook her head and shrugged. 'What if Cousin Tony doesn't want the house?'

'Why shouldn't he want it? It's a house, isn't it?'

Amy nodded, but looked unconvinced. 'He's really thinking of buying a house in Oxfordshire.'

'Where's that?' Megan wasn't too interested. It didn't matter what Amy's cousin had been thinking of doing, as long as he did the right thing now. 'Is it where they make Oxo?'

'I dunno, it might be. It's about five centimetres from the bottom of Wales on the map. But there's lots of bits of it. There's one bit where he knows someone, so that's why he was going to live there.'

'Five centimetres straight along?'

Amy nodded.

That's quite a way, thought Megan, well past Alton Towers for a start. 'How far up does it stretch?' It could be good, very good indeed, for Amy to have a cousin who lived near Alton Towers.

'Not that far. Anyway, if you're thinking of Alton Towers, we want him to buy this house, don't we?'

Megan didn't reply at once. She was thinking of the benefits of knowing someone who lived near Alton Towers. If Amy's cousin did buy a house down there, he would take Jack away. If he didn't, he'd buy this one and keep Jack here. Oh no, that wouldn't do at all. She hadn't thought of that.

'We need him to buy both.'

Amy gave her a puzzled look and Megan explained. If her cousin bought this house today, then Jack was safe from O'Neill's gun, but he would still be here. Whereas if he bought the house near the Oxo factory, he'd take Jack miles away and there'd be no more worry about swapping.

'But we need him to buy this one,' said Amy, 'or we won't be in time to stop Naylor's uncle.'

'I know. I know.' Megan clenched her fists in frustration. 'Can he buy the Oxo one afterwards?'

'I don't think he'll buy two. And anyway, I don't think they do make Oxo there.'

This needed serious thought. Jack must be kept out of the clutches of Naylor's uncle, but Megan had been banking on someone buying him and taking him far away. If Amy's Cousin Tony came to live here, she was going to have to worry about Jack every day for the rest of her life.

Footsteps crunched on the gravel. They gave each other a furtive look and crept towards the entrance. It was the old man coming to look for them. 'He said I'd find you out here. He says to tell you, you needn't wait if you don't want to. There's more to see than he'd realised. And he wants to know all about this tip.'

'What tip?'

'Yes, first I'd heard of it too. It seems the council are planning on putting a big landfill just across the way. So he'd want to know all about it, if he's thinking of buying.'

He certainly would. Megan's eyes gleamed. A tip! It was about time they had something interesting built round here instead of just more houses all the time. She hoped the owner wouldn't put up the price when she heard. Cousin Tony had said he could only just afford it.

'I've got an idea.' She turned to Amy. 'What if he buys this one this week, then sells it next week and buys the one near the Oxo factory?'

Amy stamped her foot. 'It's nothing to do with Oxo factories. And he won't. You can't just go buying and selling houses like that. Anyway, there they are, we can see what he says.'

Megan looked. There was Cousin Tony talking to someone over his shoulder. Her eyes bulged in horror as she pointed to the man walking along the path behind him. 'Who's that?' she gasped.

'He's her nephew. Old Mr Garside's niece's,' said the old man. 'He's come down to see to the particulars of the sale for her.'

Megan blinked as she puzzled it out. Old Mr Garside was the one who'd been dead for centuries, and it was his niece who was the real owner of the big house, and she was pretty ancient too from what she'd heard. So that meant that this man was her nephew … 'But he's Mr O'Neill's friend,' she burst out.

'No. He hasn't met him yet. This is his first visit. He only came down today. But I know what you mean.' The old man gave a hollow laugh. 'He's much the same sort. Shifty!'

'But he …' Megan stopped. Now she knew where she'd seen that car before. Parked out of the way behind the outbuildings that night, next to O'Neill's. But he is, she wanted to say. He has been here before, and he does know Mr O'Neill.

It was a face she would know anywhere. A face she'd been eyeball to eyeball with through the glass of the French window. A face seared on her memory along with the sight of O'Neill hiding behind the settee … and then calling for a gun.

She realised now why there'd been no fuss once she'd got away. She'd not been the only one who shouldn't have been there that night.

CHAPTER 12

Uncovering a fraud

Megan wasn't sure it was the right thing to do, but she couldn't help blurting out to Cousin Tony and the old man that she'd seen Nathan O'Neill inside the house with the man who had turned out to be Mr Garside's niece's nephew. They both looked astounded.

Amy started on an awkward question about what Megan had been doing there that night, but Megan kicked her and she shut up. She could explain to Amy when they were alone.

It was all a bit confusing. Mr O'Neill wanted to buy the big house, and the mystery man was the one organising all the business about selling it. But for some reason they shouldn't have been talking to each other that night.

'But what has he done?' Amy asked.

And Cousin Tony had embarked upon a complicated explanation about backhanders, dodging inheritance tax and bogus planning permission.

Megan, catching the term 'backhanders', wondered about tennis. Was Mr O'Neill thinking about building a tennis court on Jack's field? There might be a law about tennis courts. There were laws about all sorts of things.

'This ... er ...' She didn't want to say tennis court in case she'd got it wrong. 'Jack's field and all that. Is that what it's about?'

'Yes, of course, that'll be bogus too. New landfill! That's just to put people off. Huh, who does he think he's kidding?'

Megan could tell she'd raised a significant point and didn't want to lose the feeling of importance it gave her, so she didn't ask any more questions. And anyway it didn't matter. Mr O'Neill and Mr Garside's niece's nephew had been caught out. The old man and Amy's cousin would be able to stop him now.

'And will your friends at the Oxo factory take Jack?' she asked.

Cousin Tony gaped at her. 'My friends at where?'

'Megan!' Amy broke in. 'I've told you a million times, it's not an Oxo factory. It's because of the name,' she explained to her cousin. 'And Megan's no good at geography. She was hoping it'd be near Alton Towers.'

'I wasn't,' said Megan half-heartedly. 'But will Jack go there anyway, whatever it's called? Five centimetres from Wales?'

Cousin Tony, who couldn't seem to follow a simple conversation, gave her a strange look, then said, 'I'm going to make a few phone calls about all this. Then we'll see what's what.'

Later, as they sat side by side on the front wall outside Megan's house, Amy said, 'So everything's all right now about Jack?'

Megan nodded, but felt uneasy. Everything happened so fast. Amy's cousin was talking to all sorts of people, and Mr O'Neill wouldn't be able to buy the place. That bit seemed to be okay.

'I just feel that I daren't go anywhere near that field again,' she told Amy. 'I feel like if I get a tiny glimpse of him, we'll just swap.'

Amy tried to cheer her up by pointing out that they always managed to swap back, but Megan remained gloomy. She wouldn't be happy until Jack was five centimetres from Wales. At least Cousin Tony had promised them that much. In amongst his other phone calls, he had called his Oxo friends.

'So why didn't it work at the show?'

Megan had wondered about that herself, but they hadn't talked much about the show. It was still a sore point with Amy. 'I think it's to do with wanting to and not wanting to,' she said. 'I mean if it's an emergency, like when the vet was there, then it just happens, but it was a different sort of wanting when it was the show. Then on the way home, I didn't want to at all, and it wasn't an emergency or anything, and it just happened.'

'I didn't know about that. It'll be all right once he goes to my cousin's friends though, won't it?'

'I just hope I don't swap and end up going instead. You'll have to help out, Amy. If Jack goes and I've turned into him, you'll have to get your cousin or someone to take me to the Oxo ... to wherever it is ... so I can swap back.'

Light dawned on Amy's face. 'You can only swap when you can see each other.'

As Megan turned to reply, a large clod of earth hit the side of her head. Off balance, Megan saw Judith, Naylor's trusted lieutenant, racing down the road. 'Just you wait, Megan!' she shouted as she ran. 'Getting that man to make interfering phone calls. You just wait and see what you've got coming!'

'Judith! Come back here.'

Megan leapt to the pavement and set off in pursuit. She wasn't letting one of Naylor's cronies get away with that, and from the speed of Judith's flight, she was on her own. Judith's feelings must have been thoroughly stirred for her to strike out without Naylor there for support, especially knowing that Megan could outrun her with no trouble at all, which she did as they reached the corner.

After she'd finishing stuffing mud down Judith's collar, Megan asked, 'What are you on about anyway? You were on our side about Jack.'

Judith, red-faced and angry, seemed to be weighing up her chances if she launched another attack. Reinforcements in the person of Amy panting up alongside them decided her to hold back. 'You've only gone and wrecked Alton Towers for us all,' she muttered.

'Alton Towers?'

Megan had no idea where Alton Towers or Judith fitted into the business with Jack, but with Judith at their mercy, they would soon get to know. She saw Judith flinch. Her determination to get to the bottom of this must be showing.

Walking back beside Amy, after they'd finished with Judith, Megan shook the soil from her hair and said, 'I didn't know Naylor's uncle was taking them all to Alton Towers.'

Amy hadn't known either. They were silent for a while. Naylor got all the luck. It had been something to do with the big house. Once he'd bought it, he was going to take Naylor and her cronies out for the day as a treat, and now, according to Judith, the sale had been delayed.

'I hope it hasn't just been delayed,' she said to Amy. 'I hope it's been stopped completely.'

They hurried to Amy's to find out.

'Nothing finalised,' Cousin Tony told them, 'but the wheels are in motion. I'll let you know when you get home from school tomorrow.'

CHAPTER 13

Burger, chips and Tomato sauce

They found out before school finished the next day.

The trouble started on the school bus on the way in. No one would speak to them, but they were forced to listen to loud, indignant speeches obviously meant for their ears.

'They've completely wrecked Naylor's uncle's plans.'

'He had this big deal going through ...'

'... taking us all to Alton Towers. All Naylor's special friends ...'

Ah, thought Megan, all Naylor's special friends. Now she understood the climate of hostility they had been up against lately. Everyone who had a glimmer of a chance was sucking up to Naylor in the hope of being counted as a special friend. And that was just about the whole of the school-bussers.

Resentment simmered through the morning. Mid-lesson Megan felt a sharp prod from behind and, as she turned, her books clattered to the floor. At break-time, she and Amy kept out of everyone's way, but when they came back, Megan found her pencils snapped in two.

'At least Jack's okay,' Amy whispered.

By lunchtime, Megan was boiling with the injustice of it and ignored Amy's attempts to avoid trouble. She stood firm when Naylor tried to barge her out of the lunch queue. She sat firm too, as Naylor's crowd marched up to the table where she and Amy were sitting and said, 'Get lost, you two. We're sitting here.'

Amy started to pick up her tray, but Megan stopped her. 'We were here first. You shove off, Naylor O'Neill.'

Amy looked surprised when Naylor gave in and took her seat opposite Megan. Two of Naylor's cronies were forced to find seats at another table. Megan wasn't surprised. She knew that Naylor couldn't do much under the eye of Mr Connor who was on dinner duty, even if the kitchen staff might have turned a blind eye.

Judith sat in the chair next to her.

Megan speared a chip, but as she raised it to her mouth a nudge sent it spinning to the floor. She turned in fury. 'Just you try that again, Judith!'

'Yeah, and what …?' Naylor said from across the table.

There was a squeak from her other side. She turned to see Amy picking peas out of her lap. Several more rolled across the floor. Megan glared round the table, but they were all sitting eating, attention on their plates, faces impassive.

Mr Connor approached, walking between the rows. Peas squished underfoot. He looked down, then up at the nearby tables. The culprit was not hard to find. Amy's fork, on which reposed a single pea, still hovered midway between the plate and her mouth, 'Do be careful, Amy.' He continued on down the room. Naylor looked up and smirked.

Megan ground her teeth. She knew Amy was right to ignore them. The more you got annoyed, the worse they were. But even the thought that Jack was safe couldn't keep her calm.

Amy passed her the sauce bottle. She upended it to splat a dollop in the middle of her burger. Then, quick as a flash, Naylor leant across and crushed her hands over Megan's, squeezing with all her might. The top dropped off and a great cascade of tomato sauce covered Megan's plate, and Megan erupted.

Before Naylor could pull away, Megan had her by the hair. 'You'll be sorry for that, Naylor O'Neill.'

Hands clawed at her from every angle. Naylor struggled and hit out. Amy's quavering, 'Oh Megan,' was drowned out by the shouts from all around. Megan had a single aim and nothing was going to stop her until she had pushed Naylor's face into the inedible, tomatoey heap that had been her lunch.

The table top became a struggling mound of pulling, pushing, gasping and sputtering until a great roar snapped Megan back to reality.

'Megan Crewe! Naylor O'Neill!' the voice roared. 'The office. Now!'

Trailing along behind Naylor, knowing that big trouble awaited them both, Megan almost felt it had been worth it. Naylor was covered in tomato sauce.

Megan and Naylor sat at opposite ends of the detention room, bending furious faces over their books as Mr Connor strolled up the middle of the room towards them, then erupting into face-pulling, silent growls and mouthed threats as he strolled away. Once he wandered as far as the door and, with a fierce look to pin them in their seats, took a step out into the corridor.

Megan seized the opportunity to whisper, 'I'm glad you're not going to Alton Towers.'

Naylor glowered. 'I'll get you for this.'

Mr Connor was just visible, his attention on something at the far end of the corridor. He hadn't heard. Megan taunted Naylor again. 'And I'm glad your creepy uncle can't buy the big house.'

This time, Naylor didn't glower. She darted a look of surprise at Megan, followed at once by a sly smile.

Megan narrowed her eyes, but then Mr Connor turned and they both bent over their books.

Amy was cranky and tearful as the day finished and they trailed out across the yard. She wanted to phone her mum to come and fetch her. 'No Amy, you've got to stand up to them like I do.'

'I suppose.' Amy kicked at the ground and continued her way towards the bus queue.

There was no pushing and shoving. No loud comments. They got on with no shouted orders from Naylor about where to sit. They went to the back without a murmur from anyone. And yet it wasn't as though no one was taking any notice. Naylor suppressed a smile. There were whispered comments. Something was afoot.

Amy looked more scared than ever. Megan strained to hear Naylor.

'... their faces when they find out ...' Then a burst of laughter.

More whispering. Then Judith's voice, '... not fair really ...'

'Oh, if you want to be on their side ...' Naylor's voice returned to its usual level.

'No, I'm not,' Judith said, 'It's just that ... it doesn't seem fair to take it out on the horse, that's all.'

'It's only a broken down old nag that no one wants.'

Megan felt a creeping horror. What was going on? 'What are you talking about, Naylor O'Neill?' she demanded.

Naylor turned and gave her a big grin. 'Nothing.'

'Oh yes you are. What are you saying about Jack? Judith, what's she saying about Jack?'

Judith avoided her eye.

'She can't do anything to Jack,' Amy piped up, 'because her uncle isn't getting the house anymore.'

There were muffled guffaws. 'Oh yes, he is,' said someone.

'So you've caused all that trouble for nothing.'

'The only difference,' the nearest of Naylor's cronies turned to spit the words into their faces, 'is that we don't get to go to Alton Towers! And you're going to be sorry for that!'

They sprinted straight round to Amy's to find Cousin Tony.

'What's happened? Naylor says her uncle is still buying it.'

'Yes, but don't worry,' he said. 'He's paying a fair price now.'

'But that's not the point,' Megan wailed. 'What about Jack?' Between them they outlined the day's events.

Cousin Tony seemed unperturbed. 'Don't you worry about that. Everything's taken care of. From what I hear, that friend of yours, the old guy at the house, has had a good talk with Mrs G, and she's thinking of disinheriting the scheming nephew. Not only that, but your MacSteel is going to have to bring his dealings above board. He thought he had planning permission in the bag for some lucrative executive homes, with a fat backhander for the disreputable nephew, but his tame councillors have been in full retreat, once the little scam over the house came out. They're not too pleased about him spreading false rumours about the landfill either. But I'm not surprised his generous gesture with regard to Alton Towers is off. He won't do as well out of this as he hoped. You've done pretty well you know. You can give yourselves a pat on the back for being instrumental in foiling what might have turned into a nasty fraud.'

Megan jigged impatiently. 'Never mind all that,' she said. 'What about Jack?'

'Calm down. I told you everything's taken care of. My friends near Oxford will give him a home. They've arranged to collect him on Saturday.'

'Five centimetres from Wales.' Amy beamed. 'I told you it'd be okay.'

'When does Mr O'Neill buy the house?' said Megan.

'Turns out they were pretty far down the road with things. It was only a matter of readjusting the price. Other than that, they're sticking to timetable. Final papers will be signed on Friday. Here, have one of these.' He held out a box of chocolates towards Megan.

She gave them a glance. 'No thanks.'

Amy, open mouthed in amazement, scuttled after her as she left the room. 'Megan? Are you ill?'

'I can't fancy chocolate, Amy, not even those untidy ones. They'd be just like eating grass. It's Naylor's uncle. He's getting the house on Friday, and the people from the Oxo factory aren't coming till Saturday.'

Light dawned on Amy's face. 'Oh no.'

'Yes. We've got to keep Jack safe for a whole night.'

CHAPTER 14

Grounded

Amy looked up at her mother. She wished Megan was here. She wasn't used to arguing on her own. 'Why can't I?' she pleaded. 'It's really important.'

'Because you're grounded, Amy. I'm ashamed of you for fighting. I couldn't believe it when Mr Connor phoned. I'm beginning to think Megan Crewe's a bad influence.'

'No she isn't, Mum. And it wasn't us, it was Naylor. And it was only to save Jack, and them all going on about Alton Towers all the time.' But it was no use. Her mum was implacable. She was grounded until tomorrow, when she would be allowed out with Cousin Tony to see Jack off to his new home.

She was glad the week was over. It had been a bad one, even though it hadn't erupted into violence again after Monday. Somehow Mr Connor seemed to pop up every time Naylor and Megan squared up to each other.

'What's that black look for?' Cousin Tony came in and was settling himself down with the newspaper.

'My mum's grounded me.'

'Hmm, I heard you'd been fighting.' He opened the paper and reached for a box from his inexhaustible supply of chocolates.

'That was ages ago, and it wasn't me. I helped to stop it.' Amy shuddered at the memory. She'd found herself at the bottom of the rugby scrum of flailing bodies all struggling to drag Megan off Naylor. Then she laughed. 'You should have seen Naylor though, burger, chips and tomato sauce.'

'Uh huh,' he murmured from behind the newspaper. 'Chocolate?'

'No, tomato sauce … Oh …' Amy reached towards the box, then her hand dropped. 'No thanks.'

Her cousin looked up. 'Are you ill?'

She shook her head. 'They'd only taste like grass.'

'You're being let out tomorrow, you know. We're going to say goodbye to Jack.'

'Huh, that's all you know,' she muttered.

Even if Naylor's snide comments hadn't made it quite clear what she'd persuaded her uncle to do, Judith had told them in the end. No one was sure what catastrophe had befallen Mr O'Neill, but the things he'd had to say about broken down old cart-horses and interfering brats made no one doubt that it had been a serious one. Those who heard him had stored up several new words that they would not be using in Mr Connor's hearing.

'He's promised me that nothing'll happen to the horse,' Cousin Tony said. 'Good heavens, it's only for tonight. It's hardly going to be a bother to him to have it stand in a field for a single night. The old guy's going to be living there for a few months yet. One horse won't make a difference.'

She and Megan had discussed a plan of action. Saturday

morning was when O'Neill would act. The people from Oxford wouldn't arrive until the afternoon. Five centimetres from Wales was a long way to come. She and Megan were going to get Jack out of his field first thing and hide him … somewhere … they hadn't decided where, but Megan was sure to think of something. The bit they hadn't planned on was being grounded. Interfering Mr Connor was to blame for that!

'Can we go to see Jack off first thing tomorrow?'

'They won't arrive till lunchtime.'

'I know, but we need to go first thing, just in case. Can we?'

'What you mean is you want to go out tomorrow morning, and if you don't go with me, you won't be allowed out?'

'Yes, kind of … Can we?'

'I'll think about it.'

Further conversation was drowned by sudden pandemonium from the hall. The bell ringing, fists banging, then the door slamming open and her mum's voice, 'Megan!'

Megan burst into the room. She panted with exertion, her face tear-streaked. Her voice when she could get out the words was both breathless and full of rage. 'He's phoned me,' she gasped, gulping in great lungsful of air between words. 'The old man … He's there now … O'Neill … He's got a man with a gun … Jack …'

Amy leapt to her feet, and for once Cousin Tony understood what Megan was talking about. 'He can't do that!' he shouted. 'He gave me his word. Where's his number.'

'It's too late for the phone,' wailed Megan. 'They'd already gone into the yard to get the man's gun from his car. That's when the old man rang me.'

'Come on!' Cousin Tony grabbed his stick and headed for the door, Megan and Amy at his heels.

Megan raced ahead. Amy ran by her cousin's side. He put on quite a turn of speed despite his limp. 'Which way are we going?'

'This way. It's a shortcut.'

'Then why did you take me all that way ...?'

'It's because of swapping and things ... I'll tell you later.'

They gave their full attention to making as much speed as they could in pursuit of the more fleet-footed Megan who had disappeared round the corner of the lane.

As they reached the first corner, Megan was up ahead, almost out of sight. Then as they watched, she skidded to a halt and staggered back, slumping down on to the verge.

'Oh no!' wailed Amy racing up to her. 'It's too late.'

She stared past the slumped, forlorn figure of Megan. O'Neill and another man were striding across the field. The man had a gun slung under his arm. But where was Jack?

Cousin Tony arrived, puffing hard. He looked down at Megan. Amy saw his mouth open to speak.

'Wait!' She grabbed his arm, nearly pulling him off balance. 'It might be all right. Quick.'

A wave of relief flooded through her. She pulled Megan to her feet, ignoring her cousin's puzzled look, and hauled her towards the gate.

Megan had been eating grass.

CHAPTER 15

Jack disappears

'Where the hell is it?' stormed O'Neill, turning such a glare on Amy that she nearly dissolved in terror.

Cousin Tony squared up to him and spoke in a quiet, but firm voice. Amy, awe-struck at his bravery, couldn't follow what he was saying, but O'Neill calmed down to a sinister muttering. 'Well, if it isn't those two meddling brats, who is it?'

Now Cousin Tony struck off on a different tack. What, he demanded to know, did O'Neill think he was doing with that gun? 'We had an agreement, Mr O'Neill.'

'Agreement be damned. That nag has been causing damage, breaking through hedges.'

Amy backed off a little, pulling the lolling figure of Megan along with her. Where was Jack? Where was Megan?

'Where've you got him?' It was the old man whispering in her ear.

'I don't know. Megan's taken him somewhere.'

'Yes, but where?' The old man gave Megan's form a puzzled look. Megan's face gave him a benevolent smile and she stretched her neck out towards a tasty morsel of hedge. Amy tugged her away from it. 'I don't know,' she said again.

'What, has she just let him out to wander?' The old man's

puzzlement was deepening as he looked from one to the other of them. 'He'll just wander back again. And if they find him before we do …'

He let the sentence hang and Amy felt she could have burst into tears. What if they tracked down Jack and shot him? She looked at the blank-eyed figure beside her. 'Tell me where you are?' she whispered fiercely.

'Well it can't have gone far.' They heard O'Neill's strident tones. 'Let's try the outhouses.'

'I don't know where he can have got to,' said the old man as they all hurried after O'Neill and the man with the gun. 'He was there in the field when they left the house. I saw him with my own eyes.'

And he didn't jump the gate into the lane like last time, thought Amy, or we'd have seen him. And Megan couldn't have doubled back to the top of the field because O'Neill would have seen her. Which way would she have gone? With a sinking feeling, as she hauled Jack behind her, she realised that the only thing Megan could have done was to jump the fence into the yard. O'Neill was right. She would be hiding in one of the outbuildings.

'Get Megan to tell me where you are.' She kept her voice down so the old man wouldn't hear. Megan's eyes stared through her and she yawned. She didn't even know if Jack was capable of thinking things at Megan, wherever she was. But then Amy felt Megan's figure tense. They were close by, she was sure of it.

O'Neill slammed his way into the big barn, poking about

the old cattle stalls. Amy held her breath, wondering what she would do if she heard a shot ring out. She wanted to call out as loud as she could, to tell Megan to swap, not to risk it. It was too dangerous, even if they did lose Jack. But what would she shout? And what if Megan couldn't? And anyway … she gasped … she'd forgotten. Megan couldn't swap unless she and Jack could see each other.

She darted ahead, pushing her cousin out of the way, elbowing past the man with the gun and dragged Megan's form into the middle of the barn. She spun round, trying to see into the dark corners. She must at least give Megan a chance to swap before the gun was fired.

'Other side,' barked O'Neill, marching out.

They weren't in the big barn then. But Megan's figure kept snapping on to the alert. Amy could almost feel the fear. The real Megan was nearby, and she'd sensed the gun.

O'Neill headed for the derelict garage.

Once more, Amy pushed through, and found herself jammed in the door with him as they both tried to get in first. O'Neill gave them a look of incredulous indignation, turning his wrath automatically on Megan, whose face gave him a serene smile before blowing a gentle raspberry.

In desperation, Amy pushed her through then jumped up and down in agitation. Where was Jack? O'Neill banged his way into the old feed stores and workshops, anywhere that could conceivably conceal a horse. The man with the gun stood in the doorway.

No, still nothing. Where next?

'The forge!' said O'Neill and Amy raced out again, determined to beat him to it.

It was the lolling figure of Jack in Megan's body that was the problem. Half comatose and half wide-awake and alert to danger. It was hard to pull him along. But Amy daren't let go. And she daren't let O'Neill and the man with the gun find them without giving Megan a chance to swap.

On her own, she could have been first inside, but with a thunk of horrified disbelief she found herself and O'Neill once again wrestling together in the doorway. He gave her such a look as they burst through into the outer room of the old forge that she expected the floor to open up and swallow her.

Once again she stood between O'Neill and the man with the gun. She must give Megan the chance to make eye contact. She was running on numb terror now. She, who would take the long way round to avoid Naylor unless she had Megan with her, was standing up to Nathan O'Neill. It was too weird to be true. After today, she thought, nothing would ever scare her again.

'No, not here.' O'Neill shouldered Amy aside as he gave up his search and went to stand, perplexed, in the yard. He and the man with the gun were muttering together.

The old man hurried over to where Amy and Cousin Tony stood. 'They're saying he broke through into the garden a week or so back. They're going to look there. I don't believe it myself. He's never broken out in his life. But come on, we don't want them finding him.' The old man hurried off.

'No,' said Amy, and Cousin Tony stopped. 'He's round here somewhere. I'm sure he is.'

'I don't think he can be. They've looked everywhere.'

'But he must be. If we find him, can we take him home? He can go in the greenhouse just for tonight.'

'If we find him, we'll sort something out. But we can't possibly take him to your house. There just isn't room. You couldn't fit a horse in your greenhouse, even if your mother let you try.'

Amy stamped her foot. 'But what can we sort out? If we find him and try to talk to them, they'll shoot him.'

Cousin Tony opened his mouth to speak then stopped. He had no illusions left about Nathan O'Neill.

The old man hurried back towards them. 'You're right,' he whispered. 'He came this way. He's trampled my asparagus.'

Amy had a sudden inspiration. 'Is there an upstairs anywhere?'

'Not one that Jack could get to.'

'Show me anyway. Quick!'

They combed all the buildings again, Amy diving into corners and climbing ladders in a way that had the old man shaking his head.

There was nothing. Not a sign. Amy trailed into the yard. He must be here. But they'd looked everywhere. Every space that could conceivably contain a horse no matter how inaccessible.

And then a small whinny reached her ears.

CHAPTER 16

A Tight squeeze

Megan froze. After the panic and flurry, she thought she'd saved the situation at the last moment, and now she realised she was trapped.

Coming round that corner, she'd seen O'Neill and the man with the gun. Jack had been standing by the gate. Everything had crowded in upon her. Jack, munching away, unaware that he was tangled up in someone else's quarrel.

A brief worry, what if this time I can't ... but she could. The scene in front of her had changed to grass and mud, and at the edges of her wide field of vision, two laughing figures striding out across the ground.

Holding Jack's breath, she'd ambled his body off to one side, and the moment the hedge hid them from view, she broke into a gallop. The larch-lap fence ahead of her was quite low and she was going downhill. She leapt into the air and sailed over. 'Oof!' Something had felt prickly underfoot. Look before you leap, Aunt Ellie would have said.

She'd picked her way through the stalks, keeping half an eye out behind her. Where to now? Her first thought had been to head for the road and home, but no. She needed Amy to keep her hidden. What if someone saw Jack on his own on the road? But what was it that Amy had said last time? We'll hide him in one of the sheds. Yes, that would do. She had trotted towards the big barn.

There was shouting from behind. They were coming after her. Oh no, she was being stupid. They would look in the barn. But never mind, there were plenty of other places — the old forge maybe. Then it had struck her that anywhere she could hide Jack, was also somewhere they would look. The voices had come nearer as she'd decided she had to make for home. But she'd stopped on a gasp. The gate was shut, trapping her in the walled yard. There wasn't enough spring in Jack's legs to get him over eight feet of bricks and mortar.

She'd swung Jack's big head left and right. The barn ... the garage ... the house ... It was a vista of closed doors and of places they would be sure to look.

She'd heard the cracking of twigs and creaking of wood as they'd climbed the style. They'd be upon her at any moment.

Then she'd seen the tiny hut at the end, its windows encrusted and opaque. The door pushed open and she had tried to force Jack's body inside. She could only get half in. The open door would give her away, not to mention the vast expanse of Jack's rump and the other three quarters of his body sticking out into the yard. She eased out. There had to be somewhere else?

Oh no! This was it! They were coming for Jack with a gun. No. They were coming for her ... with a gun. Why had she swapped? Why hadn't she stopped to think?

I'm sorry Jack, she thought, we've done our best, but I'm going to have to ... The words 'swap back' hovered in her mind. She gulped. Swap back how? She didn't have a chance of swapping unless she could see herself. But she was the other side of the field ... it would mean rushing past them ... past the man with the gun. He would shoot her ...

In desperation, as raised angry voices came nearer and nearer, she backed off, bumping into the tiny shed. There was nothing else for it, she had to try. Jack's rear end squashed through the gap. She thought the wall would fall down with the pressure she was putting on it. She wished it would, it might give her the room to do something with the door.

With a final heave, she was almost inside, but with the door flat against the inner wall, she was plainly visible. There were some small shelves, the sort that might hold plant pots. She scrabbled Jack's front feet up them, sideways. If she could just stand up on his hind legs ... The ceiling wasn't high enough. It was a terrible squeeze. Her head was next to her knees. She couldn't see a thing. Feeling the top corner of the door against her head, she grasped it in Jack's teeth and scraped it painfully along his shoulder as she forced it round the bulk of his body.

It was just past the critical point when her feet lost their grip. She slithered down the tiny shelves, shattering them to splinters. The bulk of Jack's body slammed the door shut as she thumped down. So firmly did it bang into place that Megan thought it would never open again.

She barely had time or space to heave a sigh. But as long as they hadn't heard the bang of the door, surely they would never think to look in a tiny shed like this.

Head pressed into the bricks, she strained to hear. Was that O'Neill's voice raised in anger? Were those Amy footsteps racing across the yard?

She could feel Jack nearby, but it was a long time before she dared to whinny.

Amy swung round. Where had that whinny come from? There was a tumbledown bit at the end with tiny, mud-encrusted windows and a door that looked like it hadn't been shifted in a million years.

'You couldn't get a dog in there,' the old man said. 'Let alone a gentleman like Jack. That door opens inwards. He wouldn't get his nose inside.'

Amy pressed her face to the ancient glass. She could hardly see a thing. There was no light, no other window. It was tiny, some sort of minute potting shed. And yet … and yet …

'Come here!' she called. 'Quick!'

The old man hurried over and rubbed at the glass. 'Well, I'll be blowed,' he said. 'I've never seen the like.'

Cousin Tony squinted through the thick glass. The shed was filled from wall to wall with the unmistakable bulk of Jack. His rump was pressed hard against the end wall, his body and nose concertinaed up behind the door.

They managed to force the door open a crack before it wedged against Jack's solid form.

The old man's mouth hung open. 'It opens inwards, how the ...?'

'Never mind how he got in,' said Cousin Tony. 'How the Dickens are we going to get him out?'

Then they all froze. Heavy, clumping footsteps crunched down the path. Angry voices floated down to them. O'Neill and the man with the gun were back.

CHAPTER 17

A shock for Amy's mum

Megan heard the door creak as it was pushed. It opened about as far as the Oxo place was from Wales – five centimetres – and then banged into Jack's nose. Out of Jack's left eye she could see the light stream through the thin gap as first Amy's, then Cousin Tony's and then the old man's incredulous eyes peered through. I can't even try to climb up on to two legs again, she thought, I've broken all the shelves.

Then the door was pulled shut and angry voices swelled. O'Neill and the man with the gun. She heard the old man clear his throat and speak in wooden tones. 'There was a phone call, Mr O'Neill. Some people driving up the main road. They'd seen a horse trotting along.'

A quick-fire volley of questions from O'Neill, some more shouting and the roar of a car starting up.

Footsteps approached the door. No one tried to open it this time. Instead, there came a series of grunts, squeaks and creaks. Cousin Tony said some words that would have got him a detention from Mr Connor. The creaking turned to banging.

At last with a crack of splintering wood the door fell away. With difficulty, Megan disentangled Jack's head from the crumbling brickwork and forced his legs to stretch out until the all-confining walls released her and she could burst out into the yard like a cork popping from a bottle.

'We can go to our house, can't we?' Amy pleaded with Cousin Tony. 'He can easily fit in the greenhouse, and it's just for one night.'

'Well ...' Cousin Tony looked horrified as he peered at the tiny space into which Jack had been wedged.

With a cry of, 'Come on, Megan,' Amy set off at a run dragging Jack's comatose form towards the gate that now swung open. Megan was amazed. She'd never known Amy not to wait for proper permission, but she wasn't going to stand around. O'Neill might return at any moment.

The greenhouse was massive compared to the tiny shed. Megan walked Jack in and looked through the glass to see what was happening outside.

Amy panted up dragging Jack by Megan's belt. Amy looked exhausted. Jack's body felt quite exhausted too. Megan looked hard at the two figures outside, willing herself to swap back. Of course, it didn't work. Then she gave an indignant whinny and stamped Jack's feet. Amy was letting her eat leaves. Amy heard the whinny, sighed and moved Megan's form out of the danger area.

Noises from the side of the house. Cousin Tony appeared with the old man. The old man had brought a big string bag full of hay, which he tied up in front of her. 'There you are, old lad,' he said. 'Get some of that inside you.'

Megan looked at it with distaste. Her wide vision showed her the scene in the garden. Cousin Tony was holding out one of those large boxes of chocolates. Amy reached for one. Amy would eat the lot in record time, now she knew there were no Mont-thingies, and she, Megan, would be stuck out here all night with nothing but dried grass. It was all too much. She stiffened and raised her head preparatory to giving a bellow of rage.

The old man's voice came from somewhere nearby. 'Steady on, old boy,' he said. 'Don't go and have a turn in the middle of this lot.'

There was a moment of disorientation, as though she was listening to voices from far away, then she heard the old man again. 'Yes, he's settled fine now,' he said. 'There was a bit of a worrying moment, but he'll stand there good as gold till morning.'

And Megan saw a tray of untidy chocolate swim into view in front of her. A great wave of relief rolled over her. She watched her hand reach out and take two. Amy sagged with relief and let her hand fall from Megan's belt.

'Quick, let's go.' Megan was desperate to move out of Jack's line of vision.

But Cousin Tony stopped them. 'Right then,' he said. 'You promised me an explanation. Shivers down the spine ... swaps ... all that.'

Megan shared a furtive glance with Amy as she let out a sigh. They had promised, but what new trouble would this lead to? She turned her back on the greenhouse and

94

began the tale, 'It wasn't our fault, and it was all mixed up at first.'

'Yes,' said Amy. 'We didn't know if Jack liked chocolate or what.'

'Or if I was getting to like sprouts.'

'And it wasn't Jack's fault about that stone pot and breaking the hedge.'

'Then Megan said it wasn't the same sort of wanting, so that's what went wrong at the show.'

'That and his nose being so big ...'

'And you can't really get a horse to talk, except neighing and that.'

'Horses just don't belong in bedrooms.'

'And we don't know if Aunt Ellie didn't notice. We were really quick. Or if she forgot about it. Only we can't ask in case we remind her.'

'Then we got grounded.'

Cousin Tony and the old man looked from one to the other of them, like spectators at a tennis match.

'Any the wiser?' Cousin Tony said to the old man.

'Can't say I am.'

'But all's well that ends well, eh?'

A voice of thunder erupted behind them.

'What's the meaning of this?'

They spun round to see Amy's mum, white-faced, pointing a quavering finger at the horse in her greenhouse.

CHAPTER 18

Mega Trifle

Megan woke the next morning with a feeling of foreboding and reached for her phone to talk to Amy. She didn't know why she felt uneasy, because everything was okay. Amy's mum had been cranky, but she'd allowed Jack to stay. By bedtime tonight, Jack would be gone and life could return to normal.

'Yes, he's still there,' Amy told her. 'He's standing just where we left him. He's having a huge yawn. The old man's coming to check him over in a bit. Are you coming too?'

'Of course I'm not!' Really, Amy could be quite stupid at times. 'That's the last thing I want, ending up swapping just when they come to take him.'

'I hadn't thought of that.'

'Well I had. And my mum's gone and said I'm not grounded any more. I'm trying to think of something bad to do to get grounded again so she doesn't make me go and say goodbye to Jack. She thinks I want to.'

And that, Megan realised, was the source of her unease. No one would believe the real story. And if she ended up swapping with Jack at the wrong moment ... She shook her head as she trailed downstairs to find Aunt Ellie having breakfast.

'It's Jack, the horse they took you to see,' she heard her mother's voice as she entered the kitchen. 'Megan's been fond of him since she was little. He's off to his new home today. I've only just heard the full story.'

Thank goodness she hasn't, thought Megan, but she said nothing. Neither did Aunt Ellie. Her mum looked from one to the other of them, then said, 'Normally of course, Megan would have loved to go into town with you, wouldn't you Megan? But this is a bit of a special occasion.'

Hope leapt inside Megan. She felt a big smile begin to grow. Aunt Ellie always wanted to take her to town, and every time she pleaded and fought and pretended all the exotic illnesses she could dream up, to get out of it.

'I'll go into town with Aunt Ellie instead of going to Amy's,' she said.

Aunt Ellie gave a violent start, and Megan's mum nearly dropped her tea.

'It's … it's not important dear,' said Aunt Ellie. 'I quite understand that you want to say goodbye to … uh … Jack.'

'No, that's all right. It would be rude of me not to come out with you at least once when you don't visit very often.' There, she thought, that was unanswerable. That was the argument her mother used.

In vain, Aunt Ellie pleaded that she didn't mind at all. Megan was implacable. She was going into town with Aunt Ellie and that was that.

It wasn't the same as previous trips but Megan couldn't decide at first what was different. Aunt Ellie asked all the usual questions about school, but it was as though her heart wasn't in it. In fact Aunt Ellie hadn't had much to say about anything since she'd caught them with Jack in the bedroom, but she wouldn't risk mentioning that in case it reminded her.

'We could go home now, if you like,' said Aunt Ellie. 'And save the expense of lunch in town.'

Megan looked at her nonplussed. That was more or less what she always said to Aunt Ellie at this stage of the outing, and Aunt Ellie would reply, 'Oh no dear, don't think of the expense. It's only once in a while.'

Megan, feeling almost as peculiar as when she swapped with Jack, said, 'Oh no, Aunt Ellie. Don't think of the expense. It's only once in a while.'

Aunt Ellie gave her the sort of sour look that Megan recognised as one of her own, and in a sudden panic wondered if she had begun to swap with her aunt. But no, it wasn't the same feeling at all. And it wasn't her. It was Aunt Ellie who had forgotten how to behave.

Megan let Aunt Ellie choose the cafe. It was the sort only aunts could find. Questions about school had dried up.

'They're still using plates and things,' Megan said, trying to keep the conversation going. 'They probably can't afford boxes.'

'Polystyrene food cartons are a scourge,' said Aunt Ellie, showing a glimmer of her normal self.

'Yes, but it saves on the washing up.'

Aunt Ellie didn't reply and Megan couldn't think of anything else to say. Conversation languished.

After lunch, Megan asked if she could ring Amy, and listened with great relief. Yes, the Oxo people had arrived. Jack was loaded in the van and they were setting off any time now. They'd waited for Megan, but it was a long journey and they had to go.

'We can go home now if you like,' she told her aunt.

Megan felt an unaccustomed stab of gratitude. If it hadn't been for Aunt Ellie taking her to town, anything could have happened.

She led Aunt Ellie upstairs on the bus. It would lighten her drab life to show her how much better it was to be upstairs. 'Look how much you can see from up here. It's much more interesting.'

As the bus turned off the main road, it had to jockey for position with a lorry coming the other way. Megan glanced at it. A horse box, with a small side window. There was a flash of movement from inside.

She heard a tinny rattling sound ... and felt enclosed in a far smaller space than the upstairs of a bus ... there was a sensation of swaying gently on a hard floor ... a hint of sawdust in the air ...

'Oh no!' she cried, clutching out at the seat in front of her. There was no seat. She had no hands to clutch with. Her front hooves clattered on the metal floor. Sawdust billowed.

'Megan! How many times must you be told not to make a show of yourself in public? What on earth's the matter?' The stern voice drilled into her, pulling her along some invisible thread. Her hands gripped. Her eyes registered the bus windows. She held her breath. The tinny rattling had gone, replaced by the whine of the bus engine. She sniffed cautiously. It was the bussy smell of stale upholstery, but was there a hint of sawdust too? Out of the corner of her eye, she saw the tail end of the lorry disappear, and slumped back, trembling.

'That was Jack,' she said, 'in that horse box.'

Aunt Ellie explained to her mum about how she had been affected by that last glimpse of Jack. Her mum put a sympathetic arm round Megan's shoulders. 'I'm making mega-trifle,' she said, 'with chocolate on top. They waited as long as they could, Megan, but they had to go.'

'It's all right,' Megan squeaked and rushed from the room. She snatched for her phone to gabble out the whole story to Amy. 'It must have been him,' she finished. 'I smelt the sawdust!'

'Oh well, never mind,' said Amy. 'He's gone now.'

Never mind! Amy had no idea what a close shave it had been. Megan poured it all out again. 'I could feel the box round me … I could smell the sawdust!'

'Yes, but never mind that,' said Amy when she could get a word in. 'Cousin Tony says he'll take us to Alton Towers to make up for the disappointment of Jack going away.'

'Look, you've no idea how it felt to … Alton Towers?' The smell of sawdust receded.

'Yes, and he says he'll get one of those big car things and we can take four friends with us. Who shall we take? I've told him I had to decide with you, but I thought we could ...'

Megan listened to Amy's excited voice listing names.

'We'll tell them first thing Monday,' Amy went on. 'And we'll tell Naylor O'Neill where to get off too. Well, you can do that bit.'

'No, we won't,' said Megan.

'Why not?'

'We'll tell them that we're not allowed to decide until Friday evening. And we'll even say that we might invite Naylor.'

'But Megan ...'

Megan explained, and when she put the phone down, she felt well satisfied. Word would spread. A whole week opened up before her. Everyone vying for an invitation. Best seats on the bus. Shares in everyone's chocolate. No hassle from Naylor O'Neill.

And also – she jumped to her feet – mega-trifle! She hadn't registered when she'd first come in, because she'd still been shaking about that narrow escape from Jack. It wasn't even anyone's birthday. Her mum was doing it specially to make up for her disappointment.

She skipped to the kitchen in time to see her mum putting the top on the flaked chocolate. Her gaze tracked the packet on its route back to the cupboard. Maybe if she put some extra disappointment into her face her mum might get it out again and tip the rest of it on.

But who in the world could look mega-trifle in the eye and feign disappointment? She gave a big sigh of contentment.

Good old Jack, she thought, I hope I never see him again as long as I live.

ABOUT THE AUTHOR

Melodie Trudeaux loves life, books and horses. She is a creative artist with a passion for numbers and space travel. She hasn't been for a ride on a spaceship yet, but she lives in hope.

Melodie's favourite place to eat breakfast is Quincy Market in Boston; her favourite place to eat chocolate is anywhere as long as the chocolate is Belgian; and her favourite city to explore is Nairobi.

One day she would love to visit the moon, but she isn't holding her breath on that one.

Whenever Melodie can find time, she hops on to her blog and social media sites, and loves to chat. Please join her.

Melodie's website
Melodie on Facebook
Melodie on Twitter

Printed in Great Britain
by Amazon